Y0-CXG-710

**CONTRIBUTIONS
OF WOMEN**

MUSIC

by Catherine Scheader

Dillon Press, Inc.
Minneapolis, Minnesota

MAY – 1986
Codman Square Branch Library
690 Washington Street
Dorchester, MA 02124

Library of Congress Cataloging in Publication Data

Scheader, Catherine.
  Contributions of women, music.

  (Contributions of women) Bibliography: p.
  Includes index.
  SUMMARY: Presents brief biographies of five prominent
women in the field of music. Includes conductor Antonia Brico,
opera stars Beverly Sills and Leontyne Price, composer Ruth
Crawford Seeger, and violinist Dylana Jenson. Other outstand-
ing women in music are listed in the appendix.
  1. Women musicians—United States—Biography—Juvenile
literature. [1. Women musicians. 2. Musicians] I. Title.
II. Series.
  ML3929.S33   1985   780'.92'2 [B] [920]   85-6808
  ISBN 0-87518-274-7

© 1985 by Dillon Press, Inc. All rights reserved

Dillon Press, Inc., 242 Portland Avenue South
Minneapolis, Minnesota 55415

Printed in the United States of America
1 2 3 4 5 6 7 8 9 10 93 92 91 90 89 88 87 86 85

Contents

Acknowledgments

The author would like to thank the following people for their help in producing this book: Antonia Brico; Judy Collins; Joyce Holloway Barthelson; Gertrude Griffin White; Dorothy Cutler Smith; Edgar-Vincent Associates; Peggy Seeger; Barbara Seeger Perfect; Pete Seeger; Alan Lomax; Mike Seeger; George Price; Elizabeth Donegan; Ana and Lee Jenson; Lynn Beach; Kristin Neufeld; Joseph Szostak; and Edward Scheader.

Photographs reproduced by permission of the following: Dr. Herbert Axelrod, 126; Antonia Brico, 6, 14, 21, 27; Columbia Masterworks, 31; Ken Howard/San Francisco Opera, 99; © Lee Jenson, 111, 115, 119; Robert Lackenbach/San Francisco Opera, 86; Metropolitan Opera, 91, 95; Leontyne Price/Jack Mitchell, 78; San Francisco Opera, 94; Mike Seeger, 58, 64, 68, 72, 75; Shaw Concerts, 106; Beverly Sills/Ian Dryden, 56; Beverly Sills/Edgar-Vincent Associates, 32, 38, 44, 47.

Introduction

American music has come of age in this century. Among composers and performers, a new identity emerged, separate from the European traditions of earlier years. No longer do American musicians have to study abroad. In the opera houses and concert halls of Europe, American-trained performers are welcomed and acclaimed. Also, during these same years came an increasing recognition of women as serious musicians. Although female singers were always accepted, women soloists or members of major orchestras were rare.

The women profiled in this book all helped break traditional music practices. Antonia Brico dared to lead an orchestra. Beverly Sills, before she ever sang on an opera stage in Europe, had gained worldwide fame. For years, Leontyne Price dominated the stage of the Metropolitan Opera House, where, before, European singers had always been favored. As a composer, Ruth Crawford Seeger was one of the first Americans to explore twentieth-century music forms, and through her folk songs research, she made it possible for Americans to sing and perform their own music. Violinist Dylana Jenson brought home a silver medal from the world-renowned Tchaikovsky Competition, the youngest person and the first woman to win this honor in that important contest.

These fine musicians, along with the women whose lives are briefly described in "Other Outstanding Women," have enriched our lives with their achievements. They are models for other women who yearn to follow the songs of their own hearts.

CONDUCTING HERSELF WITH A PASSION

ANTONIA BRICO: Her joy in music and her determination to lead orchestras brought her an international career and an award-winning film.

The final movement of Ludwig von Beethoven's Second Symphony thundered through the darkened concert hall. As Antonia Brico led them through its final section, the musicians followed her quick, sure directions. When the last note ended, the audience stood, clapping wildly with excitement.

To shouts of "Brava!" the small, gray-haired conductor in the long-sleeved, dark blue dress bowed and smiled. Then she turned to the Mostly Mozart Festival Orchestra, inviting the musicians to join her in bowing to the cheers. Repeatedly, Antonia Brico raised her hands, giving the audience the conductor's signal to end. But the crowd, with good humor, ignored her. The cheering went on and on.

The evening had begun with the award-winning film, *Antonia, A Portrait of the Woman*, which told of Antonia's lifelong struggle for acceptance as a conductor. Following the film, Antonia herself had come onstage to conduct the Mostly Mozart Festival Orchestra.

For Antonia, the evening was a homecoming. It had been years since she had conducted for a New York audience. As conductor of the Women's Symphony Orchestra at Carnegie Hall during the 1930s, she had been well known. But that was long ago, and in between there were years of great silence. This night was part of a new beginning.

Today, a woman conductor surprises no one. However, when Antonia Brico was young, no females conducted orchestras in this country. Yet, she had wanted to become a conductor for as long as she could remember.

In Oakland, California, where Antonia lived as a child, Lakeside Park had band concerts every Sunday. In those early days of the twentieth century, women with long dresses and upswept hair strolled about the park. The pretty parasols they carried shaded them from the sun. Men in hats walked with them. Children in sailor suits and dresses played on the lawns. At concert time, everyone gathered around the small band stand.

On fine days, Antonia's foster parents took her to the park to hear the Oakland Municipal Band. All week long, the little girl looked forward to the Sunday outings. She loved the handsome musicians in their navy blue and white uniforms with their military-style caps. Best of all, she loved the band leader. His baton was a magic wand that filled the park with beautiful music. The music took her to a happy land where people said only kind things to little children and never, never hurt them.

The Lakeside Park bandshell was where the young Antonia was taken to hear the Sunday band concert.

Sundays were the bright centers of the shy little girl's dreary life. Her foster mother, a stern and moody woman, had a short temper, and often spoke harshly to Antonia. Her foster father was much kinder, but he was also afraid of his wife. In their gloomy house, music was the only joy. Antonia was glad to see her foster mother open the piano. There at the piano, the woman seemed able to forget her anger. On Sundays, the concerts calmed her, but by Monday she was her bitter self again. Antonia lived with the dread of making a mistake and being punished.

Her foster parents were the only father and mother she had ever known. Antonia believed they were her real parents. It would be a long time before she would know the truth.

One day, without warning, the woman's unpredictable ways brought an exciting surprise. Although Antonia had been punished many times for biting her fingernails, she couldn't stop. The family doctor had suggested learning to play the piano to help break the habit. Before she knew what was happening, ten-year-old Antonia had a piano teacher, a girl from across the street, who received twenty-five cents an hour for the lessons.

It was almost too good to be true, but it was true. All she had to do was practice, practice, practice. And practice was fun! No longer did she have to wait for summer afternoons in the park. She had the piano in the parlor every day, in good weather and bad.

Within a year, she played better than her young teacher. At religious meetings attended by the family each week, Antonia was asked to play the piano. She loved the looks of surprise as she put her foot down on the pedals. If she made mistakes, she went on playing so that no one noticed. She enjoyed the attention and hoped her foster parents listened to the praise.

She wanted to study with a new piano teacher, a woman visiting from Australia. But the new teacher charged a dollar an hour. At first, Antonia had little hope of becoming her student. But in the end, the foster mother relented.

The new teacher, Miss Fristrom, could enjoy afternoon tea with a cousin while listening to Antonia's practice. She heard every wrong note, and stopping in mid-conversation called out the error. Despite this unusual way of teaching, Antonia learned to play several difficult pieces.

When Miss Fristrom returned to Australia a year later, Antonia was ready for high school. Much to her delight, she found that there were many ways to satisfy her musical interests at Oakland Technical High School. During the day there were courses in the history and theory of music. After classes students could join either a band or orchestra.

Antonia signed up for both band and orchestra and took every music course she could. After learning that an older student named Joyce Holloway played the piano in the orchestra, she studied violin. Before long, she played well enough to join the orchestra's string section. Two years later, when Joyce graduated, Antonia took her place at the piano.

The band and orchestra each had an annual concert, and the highlight of the school year was a production of a musical by William Gilbert and Arthur Sullivan. All year long, special events kept Antonia busy. She studied, practiced, performed, and made new friends. The shy little girl was growing into a fun-loving but hard-working young woman.

The high school teachers helped students set goals and work toward them. Mrs. Minnie Woodward Davis, who taught music history, took a special interest in Antonia. She invited the young girl to her first concert, a performance of the San Francisco Symphony. On the night of the concert, the friendly teacher discovered that Antonia had perfect pitch, which is the ability to recognize the key in which a piece of music is played. Excited that her student had this rare gift, Mrs. Davis encouraged her to study music after she finished high school.

Antonia's secret dream was to become a conductor. She knew she must find a way to go to the University of

California at Berkeley. Her friend, Joyce Holloway, had entered Berkeley two years before. Paul Steindorf, her childhood hero from the Municipal Band concerts, was a professor there. Berkeley was only a streetcar ride away. She could live at home, paying her expenses with a part-time job. If only she could convince her foster parents!

She knew they would be hard to convince, because their plans for her didn't include college. They wanted her to work after she graduated from high school. When she begged them to understand her interest in music, her foster mother told her that she must go to work or leave their home. Antonia looked for help to her foster father, but he was silent.

For Antonia, not yet seventeen years old, it was a difficult choice. Although her home was not happy, it was the only one she knew. In those days, it was unusual for a young woman to live by herself. Yet something within kept insisting that she go to college. Making her decision, Antonia applied to the University.

Without warning, when it was clear that the young girl was determined to leave, her foster mother told her that she was not really their daughter. Antonia was shocked. Until that moment, she had no idea that they were foster parents. She pleaded to know who her real parents were, but the woman absolutely refused to tell her anything more.

Antonia moved into her rooming house in Berkeley in a daze, knowing that she would never go home again. She knew that someday, she would have to find out the truth about her real parents. For now, she had a new life to begin. At Berkeley, she found most of the students lived nearby and supported themselves. But few were as independent as Antonia. In the tiny room near the college that was her new home, she was more alone than she had ever been in her life.

She studied music and foreign languages at the university. To support herself, she played the piano in the sheet music department at Woolworth's. At the end of the school year, she worked as a waitress in a summer hotel. As soon as she had saved enough money, she bought a second-hand piano and gave lessons for twenty-five cents an hour. Because her practice at odd hours disturbed her landlords, Antonia had to move nine times in the next two years. Tired of moving so often, she looked about for a better way to earn money.

When radio was new, programs were broadcast live from the studio, and music accompanied every program. Joyce Holloway and two other friends had formed a group to play background music. Antonia joined them and played an instrument called the harmonium, which resembled a small church organ. Special keys made the sounds of oboe, flute and other instruments. When Antonia played the harmonium with the trio, listeners of radio station KGO in Berkeley, where the women worked, thought they were hearing a full orchestra.

Antonia had classes with Paul Steindorf, who took an interest in his talented student. Professor Steindorf gave her private lessons and invited her home for dinner every week. The Steindorfs made her feel like one of the family. Everyone helped prepare dinner, and Antonia's job was grinding the coffee. In that warm and loving home, she found the support she'd missed in her own.

She longed to tell Professor Steindorf of her dream of becoming a conductor, and finally, she got up her courage. His response surprised her. Teaching was possible, he told her, and if she was very fortunate, performing

Paul Steindorf, one of Antonia's earliest music teachers and friends.

in an orchestra. But conducting? Impossible! Her dream could never come true, he said, because she was a woman!

Nevertheless, Antonia did not give up hope. She decided to take one step at a time. She believed that if what she wanted was worthwhile, and if she worked hard enough, she would reach her goal. The first step came in her fifth year at Berkeley, after she received her college degree. She had stayed the extra year to study with the well-known pianist, Sigismund Stojowski. Stojowski had come to Berkeley for one year to teacher master classes. He urged her to study with him in New York the following year.

Antonia accepted the invitation and moved to New York to live with the Stojowski family. She helped with the children, taught piano lessons to earn money, and attended every concert that she could. She also made new friends, among them Gertrude Griffith White and her husband, John.

While in New York that year, Antonia first contacted her own real family. Before leaving California, she had made many trips to the bakery where her foster father worked. After waiting for him to finish work, she walked with him part of the way home. Each time, she begged him to tell her what her real name was. Finally, he gave in, and the next time they met he brought her birth certificate.

She learned that her real name was Antonia Brico and that she had been born in Holland in 1902. Then through a friend of Mr. and Mrs. White's, who knew people in Holland, she contacted her grandfather, an art dealer who lived in Amsterdam.

In letters from him she learned that her father had been an Italian pianist. He had gone back to Italy and no one had heard from him again. Her mother, unable to take care of her and work at the same time, had left Antonia in the care of foster parents.

In 1907, the foster parents told her mother they were taking the five-year-old on a short visit to South Africa. Instead, they came to America, settled in California, and never returned. Shortly after their departure, Antonia's mother became ill and died.

For years, her grandfather had tried to locate her. But no one he contacted in South Africa had ever heard of the foster parents. His only hope was that they would return some day with his granddaughter. Now, when he had almost given up, he heard from Antonia herself. He told her about her aunts, who were her mother's younger sisters, and Antonia wrote to them, too.

Antonia's work with Stojowski made her more determined than ever to become a conductor. She hoped to do what all young musicians dreamed of at that time—to study in Germany, the land of Beethoven. Even though her friends in New York tried to discourage her, she made her plans. She had enough money saved to last the first few weeks in Germany. Moreover, she could speak the language, and believed she would be able to give piano lessons to German youngsters.

Stojowski and her Berkeley instructors wrote letters to Karl Muck, the conductor of the Wagner Festival at Bayreuth, Germany. These letters praised Antonia's talent and ability to work hard, and convinced Dr. Muck to accept her as a pupil.

When she arrived in Germany, Dr. Muck welcomed her warmly. Despite his busy schedule, he made time for private lessons and spent hours talking with her about music. Charmed by this young American woman who sensed the deep meanings of the great composers, he admired her spirit. When Antonia told him she wanted to conduct, Muck was not surprised. Because of her understanding of the music written by Beethoven and other composers, he believed she would convince other musicians to follow her.

Dr. Muck urged Antonia to apply to the Master School of Conducting at the Berlin Academy of Music. Nineteen other musicians also applied to the school, which had very strict standards. Antonia worried for weeks that she might not be accepted, but word finally came—she was one of the two successful candidates! In

1928 Antonia became the only woman and the only American at the school.

During the two years that she attended the Academy in Berlin, she traveled to Hamburg every second weekend for private lessons with Karl Muck. To get there, she had to sit up an entire night on an unheated train. In Hamburg, she had her lesson with Dr. Muck and attended the concert of the Hamburg Symphony. By Monday morning, she was back in Berlin for her first class. For Antonia, the long trip home was a small price to pay. In return, she studied with the great conductor and met other musicians who came to the Hamburg Symphony concerts.

In 1930 Antonia graduated from the Master School. Just ahead, on February 11, was her world debut, her first public performance with a professional orchestra. Antonia planned the program carefully. She was excited that a well-known singer had been hired to perform with the Berlin Philharmonic.

Three days before the concert, however, the singer failed to appear for practice. Confident about the rest of the program, Antonia worried about the singer's part. Anxiously, she waited to hear from her. Several times she visited the woman's apartment, but no one was home.

Finally, the singer returned home. She was exhausted after spending the weekend with her lover, she told Antonia, and she would not be able to perform at the concert. Antonia gasped. It was her world debut! The singer had a very important part in the program, Antonia reminded her. The woman yawned and told Antonia that she didn't understand what love could do.

Antonia was shocked. She knew that nothing, not even love, could stop her from keeping a promise. Hurriedly, she had to arrange for a student from the Master

School to play a Schumann piano concerto which the orchestra knew.

As she stood facing the musicians on the night of her world debut, February 14, 1930, Antonia put the singer out of her mind. Her childhood dream had come true. She was a conductor, leading this great orchestra with all her energy and skill. The debut was a triumph. The musicians didn't seem to notice that their conductor was a tiny, slender, young American woman. She gave them the direction they needed to bring forth their best performances.

The music critics, who write about performances for newspapers, sent stories about the new conductor across the Atlantic Ocean to America. In California and New York, Antonia's friends read the news of her debut the next morning. Soon after the debut, they were making plans for her homecoming.

When she returned to the United States later that year, her former teachers surprised her with an invitation to conduct the San Francisco Symphony. But even before that event could take place, she received another invitation to lead the Hollywood Bowl Orchestra. The Bowl concert came first, and was her American debut, her first public performance with an orchestra in her own country. Her old friend from high school and college, Joyce Holloway, helped her to prepare for the concerts.

The American critics welcomed the new conductor. Antonia had succeeded even more than her teachers had hoped. They had believed in her ability to become a very good piano or violin player. But she had succeeded in something few people would have attempted. There had been no model for her to follow. Instead, she became the model.

A year after her debut, she returned to Germany, this time to become the first woman to conduct Karl Muck's Hamburg Symphony. Another Berlin concert occurred in that same year. As time passed, however, Antonia found it hard to keep working. The Great Depression, which had begun in 1929, affected people all over the world. Many people were out of work and had no money to spend for entertainment. In addition, Adolf Hitler was in power in Germany, and non-Germans were unwelcome on concert stages. In the end, Antonia ran out of money completely and had to ask friends to pay her way home.

New York was not much better. Antonia rented a small room for ten dollars a week, gave piano lessons to support herself, and followed the concert news in the papers. She was not alone. Everywhere, musicians were out of work. Luck, rather than ability, often determined who was working.

One night, Antonia's luck began to change. She read that Arturo Toscanini, the famous conductor, was appearing at Carnegie Hall. Deciding that she must see him, she bought a fifty-cent "walk-in" ticket at the door. As she made her way to her seat, several important people who knew Antonia from her earlier concerts and from her picture in the newspaper greeted her. Later in the evening, she was introduced to Olin Downes, the music critic for the *New York Times.*

When Mr. Downes learned that she was not working, he told her about a project for unemployed musicians that his wife was planning with a group of other women. The women had formed the Musicians' Symphony Orchestra to perform concerts at the Metropolitan Opera House. Through Mrs. Downes, Antonia was hired by Mrs. Prince, a supporter of the orchestra, to conduct the first concert.

Mrs. Prince took Antonia to a dressmaker who designed a conducting outfit for her. It was like a tuxedo, the black suit that male conductors wear, and was made of velvet. It had a long skirt and with it, she wore a white, ruffled blouse.

Hearing that a young woman would be conducting at the Met, newspapers sent reporters to interview Antonia. Although it was a new experience, she was not frightened. She answered their questions with good humor, realizing how unusual she seemed. When she spoke about the music, the reporters knew she was a serious professional.

Because Mrs. Prince worried that the Brico name by itself might not bring a good attendance at the concert, she had asked Antonia to promise to sell $500.00 worth of tickets. Antonia hadn't the slightest idea how she could sell that many tickets, but she agreed, knowing her friend Gertrude White would help.

Mrs. White spoke to the headmasters, or principals, of two private schools near her home in Greenwich, Connecticut. Happy to have their students see a female conductor, they filled several boxes at the Met. Even Mrs. Downes was surprised at the turnout. When she hired Antonia for a second concert, there was no need to ask for a promise of ticket sales.

Ticket sales for the second concert were good, and once again, the critics praised Antonia's performance. When a third concert was planned, she was again asked to conduct. However, a male singer, with whom a contract had already been signed, refused to perform with a woman conductor. A star performer, he was jealous of

Antonia became a well-known guest conductor in the 1930s.

the attention Antonia had received from the press. With regret, Mrs. Downes had to replace Antonia.

The Metropolitan Opera House concerts were a turning point in Antonia's career. Although conducting jobs were rare in the middle of the Great Depression, she received invitations from other cities. Closer to home, she had more regular jobs. She directed choral groups, gave lectures, coached singers, and instructed piano students.

For some time, she'd had the idea of forming a women's orchestra. One day, while working with a small group of women, she told them of her idea. "If nine of us can work together, why not ninety? Even in the best of times, it's hard for a woman to join a symphony orchestra. Now that jobs are scarce, it's worse. Why not form an orchestra of our own?"

Though doubtful, the other women were willing to try. They placed a newspaper advertisement for tryouts. In the meantime, Antonia asked for support from several important people, including Eleanor Roosevelt, the wife of the president. Over a hundred female musicians came to try out. It was easy to form a full orchestra.

Beginning in 1935, the group performed in New York for the next four seasons. During those years, it became part of the concert life of the city. Leading newspapers reviewed its programs and ran stories about the musicians. Readers learned about the musicians' studies, lives, and style of dress. Audiences looked forward to the concerts. They liked to see the tiny, attractive conductor with the short, waving hair come onstage and bow. She looked almost too fragile to be a conductor. But when she faced the orchestra, the audience saw her strength. She conducted with force and energy, leading the orchestra in difficult pieces.

Antonia moved into an apartment near Carnegie Hall and bought two grand pianos. There, she gave master classes in conducting, in the way she herself had learned in Berlin. Her friend from California, Joyce Holloway, came to New York to learn conducting under Antonia's direction. She soon became the assistant conductor of the Women's Symphony Orchestra.

Antonia continued to study the great music, learning longer and more difficult pieces. She formed a close friendship with Olin Downes, the most famous of American music critics. In planning programs, she discussed the works of favorite composers with Downes. Together, they explored the different ways these pieces had been played over the years. Antonia knew that the more she learned about the music and the musicians, the richer her conducting would be.

At Downes' urging, she planned to visit Jean Sibelius, the great Finnish composer, on one of her regular trips to Europe. In his native country, Sibelius was a national hero. Years before, the Russians had tried to make Finland part of their own nation. At that time, Sibelius composed stirring music based on Finnish folk rhythms that aroused people to defend their homeland. Downes told Antonia that Sibelius was loved and honored in his country the way athletes and movie stars are in America.

Knowing that the composer lived in a quiet retreat with his family, far from the large cities, Downes wrote to him, introducing Antonia. He asked the composer to have a message waiting for her in Helsinki when she came there in September.

But when she arrived, there was no message. Antonia had to decide whether to continue on her trip or try to see Sibelius without an appointment. Knowing she would regret not trying, she began the complicated journey to his home. Unable to speak Finnish, she had to find someone who understood English and could give her directions.

At the entrance to Sibelius's home in Järvenpää, she once again had doubts about coming as an unexpected guest. But as soon as she saw the tall, broad-shouldered man with the kind smile, she knew she had made the right decision. In German, he welcomed her to his home and family and apologized for having misunderstood the date of her trip.

Antonia returned to the house at the edge of the forest many times. Between visits, she studied Finnish so that she could speak to the composer, his wife, and his five daughters in their own language. Friendship with Sibelius enriched her knowledge of his music. She included Sibelius compositions in the Women's Symphony Orchestra programs. He told her that she directed his music in the way he had meant it to be played.

In the meantime, the Women's Symphony Orchestra continued to perform each season in New York, demonstrating that female musicians were the equal of men. Believing that the issue was ended, Antonia became concerned that the orchestra contributed to the separation of women. She decided to form a mixed group of men and women in its place. In 1939, she introduced the new Brico Symphony, made up of eighty musicians, of whom twenty-five were men. However, the mixed orchestra did not create enough interest to attract large audiences. After one season at Carnegie Hall, it, too, was disbanded.

When the Brico Symphony dissolved, Antonia continued to appear as a guest conductor with leading orchestras throughout the country. World War II stopped her trips abroad. Sometimes foreign musicians who were invited to appear in the United States were unable to leave their war-torn countries. One day Antonia's manager called her with an offer. Could she take the place of a conductor who had been hired by the Denver Symphony, but could not get out of his country? It might be more than a single concert, her manager told her, because the symphony wanted to hire a full-time conductor.

Antonia's appearance as guest conductor was successful and she was immediately considered for the position as the orchestra's regular conductor. The concert's success made her confident about her chances. Denver and its climate appealed to her, and she was impressed with the city's support of its orchestra. Acting on an impulse, she moved to Denver.

Antonia did not get the job. The symphony's board of directors didn't want a woman leading its orchestra. Moreover, Antonia's fame as a master teacher worked against her. Fearing she would take away their best students, Denver's music teachers did not support her.

But since she had settled in Denver, Antonia decided to stay. Once again she busied herself as a teacher and voice coach. Like other musicians, she needed to practice her instrument. For a conductor, whose instrument is the orchestra, this is not so easy. Antonia became conductor of the Denver Businessmen's Orchestra, a semi-professional group that was later renamed the Brico Symphony in her honor.

The musicians in the Businessmen's Orchestra, both men and women, worked at other jobs during the day. Although serious about their music, they were not paid salaries, as are members of a professional orchestra. They practiced with their conductor every week and performed two concerts a year.

Antonia continued to accept the few invitations she received as guest conductor. She knew she had to find a way to promote herself more effectively. She decided to ask musicians she knew to write letters of recommendation for her. Sometimes, a musician can persuade an orchestra that someone should be given a chance by writing a letter recommending the other musician's ability.

Artur Rubinstein, the well-known pianist, understood her problem when she talked to him one day after a concert in 1944. But he would have to see her conduct, Rubinstein said, before he could write a recommendation. Unfortunately, Antonia had no upcoming contract.

Someone else might have given up the idea of securing Rubinstein's recommendation, but not Antonia. Instead, she contacted a friend in New York whom she knew could hire a group of musicians, rented Carnegie Hall, and invited Rubinstein to come.

Rubinstein came, and so did Bruno Walter, a well-known conductor. Her skill and spirit impressed the two men. They both wrote fine recommendations for her. Their letters led to a number of conducting jobs in Finland, Yugoslavia, England, and her native Holland in 1946.

She continued to fill her life with old and new friends. Antonia had long admired Dr. Albert Schweitzer. The world-famous doctor, best known for his hospital in Lambaréné, Gabon, on the west coast of Africa, was also a scholar and a musician. Antonia had read his writings about the music of Johann Sebastian Bach.

Antonia and Dr. Albert Schweitzer, with whom she had a warm friendship.

Although the doctor traveled little beyond the trips he made to his home in Alsace, France, he agreed to come to Aspen, Colorado, in 1949. The occasion was a celebration of the two-hundredth anniversary of the birth of Johann von Goethe, the great German poet. A number of important people in Colorado had promised to make a large contribution to the Schweitzer hospital. In return, Dr. Schweitzer agreed to give a series of lectures on the life and work of Goethe.

Antonia attended the lectures. Later she decided to go backstage to introduce herself to Dr. Schweitzer. He was delighted to hear her speak German, and marked her copy of the Brahms' Chromatic Fantasy and Fugue with his own notes. In addition, he invited her to visit his family home later that summer in Alsace. This visit led to five trips to the hospital village in Lambaréné, where Antonia worked in the hospital community.

Each evening when the day's work at the hospital was done, Dr. Schweitzer opened his special piano. Given to him by the Bach Society in 1913, it was made with organ pedals and lined with zinc to keep termites from eating the wood. As Schweitzer sat at the piano, Antonia and he would discuss Bach. From time to time, he would play a few bars of music. When the time came to go home to America, Antonia felt that she was leaving a very special world. Only knowing that she would come back again made it possible for her to depart.

Apart from her trips to Africa and Europe each year, Antonia spent most of her time in Denver. Her energies went into symphony rehearsals, concerts, and music lessons. She had never married nor had children of her own. Instead, her students became her children, and she gave them the love and tenderness that she had lacked in her own childhood. When they became teenagers, she encouraged their development as human beings and as artists, the way her own teachers had done for her. In time many of the students who came to her small white house with its blue shutters became professional musicians themselves. News of their progress reached her from all over the world.

One student, Judy Collins, had studied piano with Antonia for six years before she turned to the guitar. During the 1960s, Judy became a popular folk singer. She sang about peace and people's rights. But she never forgot her piano teacher.

Antonia was the first woman that Judy had known who worked and supported herself. The younger woman wanted others to know this great teacher. She knew that Antonia was almost forgotten outside the western city that was her home. To tell Antonia's story, she first thought of writing a magazine article. Then she decided on a documentary film that would tell the true story of Antonia's life. With Antonia's permission, Judy made plans with Jill Godmilow, a film editor. They decided to interview Antonia and combine this material with scenes of lessons and rehearsals with the Brico Symphony.

A natural storyteller, Antonia spoke freely of her experiences in the world of concert music. She expressed her heartache over the unfairness toward women.

"I do four concerts a year," Antonia told Judy in the film. "I could do four a month. When I see the names of conductors performing overseas, it makes me sad! In other countries, women conduct major orchestras."

While some parts of the movie were sad, others were funny. Antonia's eyes sparkled when she joked about the foolish attitudes people used to have about women.

Antonia, A Portrait of the Woman, was chosen the best documentary film of the year in the New American Filmmakers Series. Antonia was surprised at how popular the movie became. She told her friend Gertrude White that she thought it would be shown only in schools. "Maybe I said too much," she told Gertrude.

"You were yourself, Antonia," replied Gertrude, firmly. "That's why everyone likes it. You're so honest about yourself that people get to know you quickly. That's what happened in the film."

Newspaper stories following the film's release brought her nationwide attention for the first time in decades. She began to receive requests for lectures and conducting appearances. Her calendar would be filled for years. She accepted them all, happy to be busy at last.

During the summer following the film's opening, she was hired to lead the Mostly Mozart Orchestra in Lincoln Center for the Performing Arts, where the new Metropolitan Opera House now stands in New York City. The concert sold out at once, and Antonia agreed to perform the program in a second concert a week later. On the second night, Judy Collins joined Antonia in accepting the standing ovation.

For Antonia, the film's success was another turning point in her career. Since then, she has crisscrossed the country, conducting the great orchestras with all her old energy and skill. But no matter where she is, she keeps one date regularly. Each Thursday evening, she returns to Denver to conduct the rehearsals of the Brico Symphony, in thanks for its members' support during the years when they were her only instrument.

In addition to her conducting appearances, Antonia is in demand as a guest speaker. On college campuses,

Antonia became a popular lecturer after the film of her life brought her nationwide attention.

students come to listen to the short, stocky woman with the comfortable manner of a grandmother. She encourages them, as grandmothers do, but challenges them to take risks. She urges young people who are gifted to choose careers in the arts. If they have talent, they will only be happy if they use it, she insists.

"Study hard, so you can use your gifts," she tells them. "Then, when the chance comes, you'll be ready. Is it a sacrifice? Will you have to give up pretty clothes and good times? Of course you will! You'll sacrifice these things that others value. But the cost is small compared with the reward you'll have. Your reward will be doing the work you love."

HITTING THE
HIGH NOTES

BEVERLY SILLS: Her stellar talent and warm, open personality made this singer one of the most popular stars of the opera stage.

The bright-eyed little girl with bouncing blond curls and dimples had been traveling with her mother for an hour and a half. They had taken a bus, a trolley, and two subway trains from Brooklyn to Manhattan, the heart of New York City. Finally, they had arrived at the apartment of the famous Estelle Liebling.

Miss Liebling was a voice teacher; opera stars such as Maria Jeritza had been among her pupils. Since she wanted the best, Shirley Silverman brought her daughter Beverly all the way to Manhattan to see Miss Liebling. Seven-year-old Beverly wanted to be a singer.

Beverly's heart was pounding with excitement as her mother rang the doorbell. Then the door opened and she and her mother were asked to come in. Beverly waited impatiently while her mother spoke to the teacher. She was so looking forward to singing the aria, or song, that she had prepared for this occasion.

Something was wrong, Beverly realized. Miss Liebling was saying that she had made a mistake: that she thought Mrs. Silverman, not Beverly, wanted to take lessons from her. Miss Liebling said she didn't teach children.

Mrs. Silverman looked as disappointed as Beverly felt. She had made the appointment, she explained to Miss Liebling, because the teacher had coached Mrs. Silverman's favorite singer, Amelita Galli-Curci. Almost from the time Beverly had been born, the child had listened to Galli-Curci's arias on records. By now, she could sing all twenty-two of the songs. And she was only seven!

Miss Liebling was charmed by the attractive woman and impressed with her strong love of music. After such a long trip, it seemed cruel to send them home without hearing the child sing. Suddenly, Miss Liebling changed her mind and invited them into her music studio. In the room where she worked with her famous pupils, the teacher led the girl to the center of the oriental rug and sat down at the grand piano to accompany Beverly.

Beverly sang "Il Bacio," an aria that she'd performed on a radio show and in special children's programs in which she'd appeared. A round of applause was the usual response when she sang, but this time, as she finished, Miss Liebling burst out laughing! Hurt and puzzled, Beverly began to cry.

Miss Liebling explained to Beverly some time after that first meeting why she had laughed. To learn her aria, Beverly had listened to records and had memorized the sounds of the foreign language. However, the girl had no idea of what the words meant, and thus sang the song as she would any nonsense syllables!

Even though Beverly didn't know Italian, Miss Liebling was impressed with her lovely, high, sweet soprano voice. While Mrs. Silverman was comforting Beverly, the teacher came to a decision. If the Silvermans were willing to make the long trip from Brooklyn for lessons, she told them, she would accept Beverly as a student.

Thrilled as she was to study with the famous voice teacher, Beverly was already used to taking lessons and singing in public. Every Saturday, Beverly attended a private school in Brooklyn where singing, dancing, and speech lessons were taught. In many families, children customarily take music and dancing lessons. Even if the children never performed, their parents believed that the training would help them appreciate music.

The best students at Beverly's school took part in "Uncle Bob's Rainbow Hour," a program broadcast over radio station WOR in New York City. In the 1930s, radio was as popular as television is today. Almost every family owned a radio and listened to certain programs regularly. It was fun for Beverly to know that thousands of people were hearing her perform.

Beverly had also gotten to sing at a restaurant in Manhattan. A film director heard her there and asked her to sing in an educational film called *Uncle Sol Solves It*. By that time the young singer became known as Beverly Sills. A name change from Beverly's real name, Belle Silverman, was suggested by a friend of her mother's. They thought Beverly Sills sounded more professional for a potential star.

All of this was a lot of success for young Beverly

from Brooklyn. She had been born on May 25, 1929, and lived with her family in a house in the Sea Gate section of the borough, not far from Coney Island. She had two brothers, Sydney and Stanley. Sydney was five years older than Beverly; Stanley was three years older. The three were close enough in age to enjoy doing things together. The two boys would go to the movies with their sister Bubbles, as she was nicknamed, or they would all go to Ebbetts Field to watch the then-Brooklyn Dodgers play baseball. The boys always looked out for their sister—they even reminded her not to cheer so loud at baseball games, because it might hurt her voice!

Beverly's father was the assistant manager of an insurance office. In the Great Depression of the 1930s, anyone who was working felt fortunate. Morris Silverman had a good job and provided a comfortable life for his family. They owned their own home, instead of renting like many people they knew, and even had money for extras like music lessons for the children.

With jobs so hard to get, few wives and mothers worked outside their homes in the 1930s. Beverly's mother could therefore devote much time to her family. Beverly remembers that her mother was always cooking or sewing. Mrs. Silverman supported all her children's interests and abilities, encouraging their best efforts at whatever they attempted. However, she loved opera, and therefore took special joy in Beverly's singing.

From Monday to Friday Beverly attended public school near her home. On Saturday, her mother took her into Manhattan to Miss Liebling's studio and then to piano and foreign language lessons before lunch. In the afternoon the two of them often saw a movie, and later might join the rest of the family for a Chinese dinner. On

Sundays, Mrs. Silverman and Beverly would travel again to Manhattan for Beverly's performance in a famous radio program.

After Beverly had been studying with Miss Liebling for two years, the teacher had decided to show off her student's training. Miss Liebling knew Major Bowes, who had a popular radio program on CBS, "Major Bowes' Amateur Hour." Beverly performed on this show, where she sang "Caro nome," an aria from Guiseppi Verdi's opera *Rigoletto.* (By then she had learned some Italian and could sing the words with meaning.) After that, Major Bowes offered her a job on his "Capitol Family Hour," a Sunday evening show heard by people all over the country. On the show she would sing and then chat with the Major. Her talent and cheerful disposition made her a favorite on the program.

Beverly enjoyed her radio experiences. She recorded a commercial for Rinso White, a laundry soap. She sang with the Morton Gould orchestra when it replaced Major Bowes' Family Hour in 1940. Soap operas on the radio were also popular, and Beverly joined the cast of "Our Gal Sunday" for a year. In it she played the part of a mountain girl whose voice is discovered by a famous opera star visiting from the city.

By the time Beverly was twelve she could travel to Manhattan by herself every Saturday for her lessons. Her parents were still in favor of the lessons, but they were concerned that her radio work took up too much time. They decided that she should give it up and concentrate on school work and her Saturday lessons. In addition, her piano teacher was urging her to take her piano studies seriously.

But Beverly had a secret dream: to become an opera

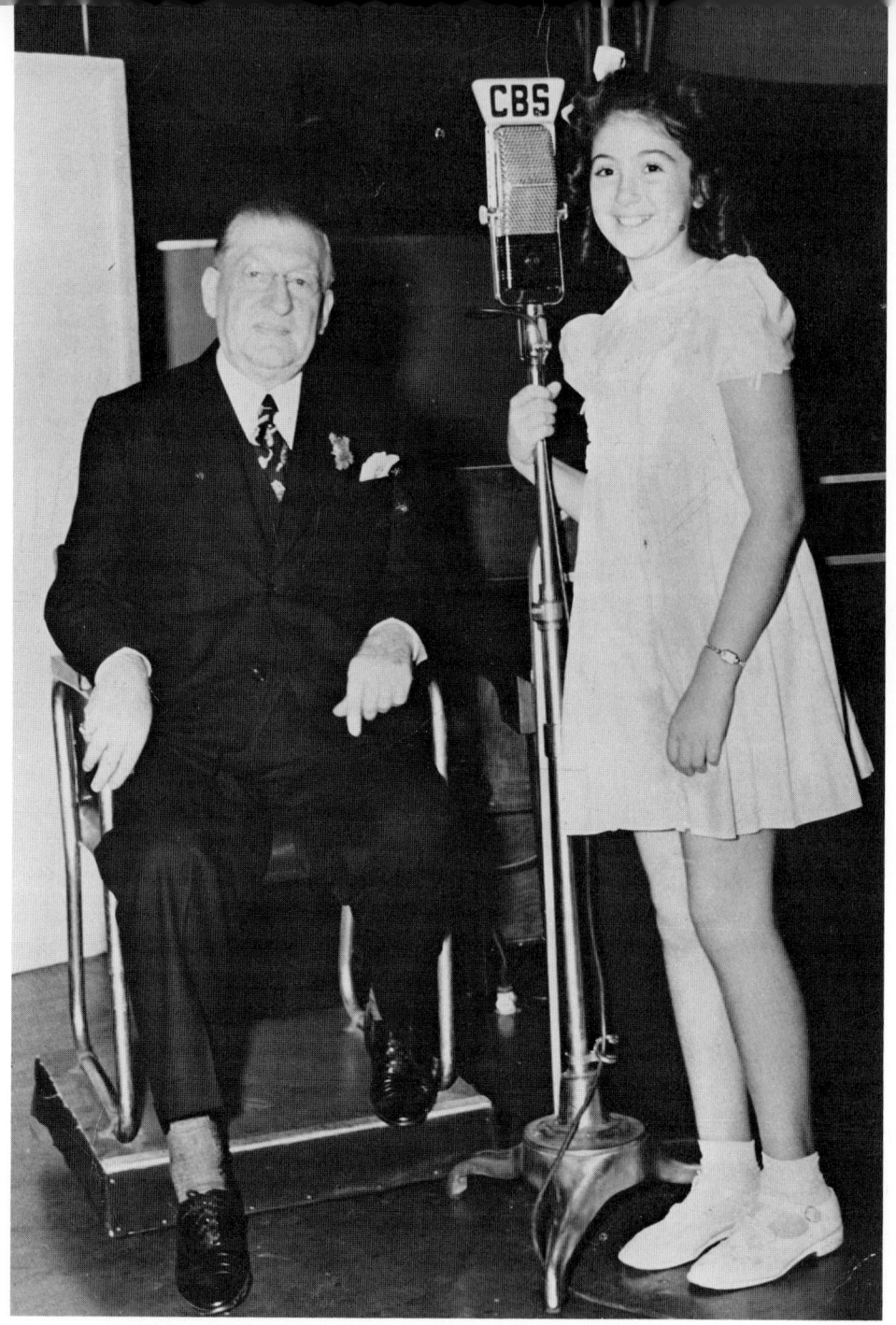

Beverly was a regular performer on two radio programs hosted by Major Bowes.

star. At age eight she'd seen her first opera, Leo Delibes' *Lakme*, at the Metropolitan Opera House. Lily Pons, who sang the title role, made a lasting impression on her. The opera was like a fairy tale that had come to life. Its colorful scenery, glamorous costumes, and interesting story lit Beverly's imagination. Afterward, she wrote to Ms. Pons telling her how she'd loved her singing. The soprano responded by inviting the Silvermans to a concert at the famous Carnegie Hall. From that time on, Beverly was a fan of Ms. Pons, collecting her records and imitating her high, light soprano singing voice.

Seeing Lily Pons in various roles gave Beverly the desire to know about the characters she was playing. Mrs. Silverman bought Beverly a book of opera stories that added to her enjoyment of the music. Instead of just listening to records and singing the arias from operas, Beverly read and thought about how each character would behave and feel.

To become an opera singer, Beverly needed to learn the languages in which operas are written. Fortunately, she had a gift for this. As a youngster she imitated the family maid, who was French, and picked up that language. At the age of ten she could speak Italian. Her father was very proud of her language ability; for Mr. Silverman, her accomplishments were signs of a good education. He wanted all his children to become broadly educated, and encouraged his sons and daughter to read and study as much as they could. But while he was interested in Beverly's singing, he never expected that she would become a public performer.

Miss Liebling also helped Beverly understand the importance of the story of each opera. For example, before she taught Beverly the role of Gilda in *Rigoletto*, she had her student translate the whole opera from Italian into English. As she learned each new role, Beverly herself did similar exercises in order to completely understand how the story was related to the music.

Estelle Liebling always took a special interest in Beverly. When Beverly was young, Miss Liebling would fill a special cup with hot chocolate to warm her after the long trip into Manhattan. She became a second mother to Beverly, and prepared her for a life in the world of music. The teacher, a former singer herself, entertained Beverly with stories of her own performances at the leading opera houses. Many of Miss Liebling's friends were noted singers; through inviting Beverly and her mother to dinner parties, Miss Liebling introduced them to these singers. Sometimes Beverly was asked to sing during these evenings by the proud teacher.

Miss Liebling's fees were high, and therefore her time was valuable. A measure of her regard for Beverly is the fact that, from the beginning, she refused to take money for Beverly's lessons. In the thirty-four years that the two women worked together, the lessons were a gift freely given.

The teacher chose opera roles suited to Beverly's stages of vocal development. At fifteen, the young girl knew twenty operas and was sure that she wanted to become an opera singer. However, she knew her goal would be difficult. Unlike today, when large cities have more than one major opera house, and regional opera companies are everywhere, there were few companies then. The Metropolitan Opera House in New York and European opera houses like the famous La Scala in Milan, Italy were the places where opera was performed. Also, large companies preferred European singers to

American singers. A young, American girl with no experience could not approach large companies like these.

To gain experience, some singers took jobs in musical plays. Often, choruses were used in these musicals. With Miss Liebling's encouragement, Beverly tried out for Broadway shows. These auditions gave her experience in singing from a stage and in making her voice heard.

Although a number of Broadway producers offered chorus jobs to the tall, attractive girl, Beverly turned them all down. To her, it seemed a long way from a Broadway chorus to the stage of an opera house. But finally, after many auditions, one offer excited her. She was asked to be the understudy for the star of a new musical being produced by the famous J. J. Schubert. If the star became ill or could not perform, Beverly would take her place.

When she broke her good news to the family, Mr. Silverman was shocked. He told Beverly she must finish high school and get a college degree. Once she had a good education, he said, she could do anything, even sing if she chose. But first things first!

After Beverly turned down J. J. Schubert's offer, Miss Liebling brought her to meet the producer himself. Although he respected Mr. Silverman's objections, Schubert hoped to persuade him to permit his talented daughter to sing in one of his plays.

At last, Beverly's father gave in and allowed her to go on tour with a Schubert company that performed musical plays written by William Gilbert and Arthur Sullivan. However, before they would give their permission, Mr. and Mrs. Silverman insisted that a member of the company be assigned to look after Beverly.

Before she left New York, Beverly transferred from Erasmus High School in Brooklyn to the Professional Children's School in Manhattan. The school, which adjusted its schedule to students who had to practice and perform during normal school hours, also gave classes through the mail. Using this mail method, Beverly managed to complete her high school program while she was on tour.

After graduation from the Professional Children's School, Beverly was offered a college scholarship to study mathematics. She turned it down, although she knew her father would be disappointed. Beverly had decided that college would not make her a better singer. On the Gilbert and Sullivan tour she became convinced that she must keep singing to improve. She could now project her voice to make herself heard and she had learned timing and moving about on the stage. She was ready to work hard and get more experience.

J.J. Schubert had another tour going out, and Beverly was again included. This time she sang in two of the three plays performed by the traveling company. In *The Merry Widow* by Johann Strauss she had her first experience in a leading role. She had a lot of fun with her role, creating a character quite different from herself.

Beverly might have continued to sing in musical plays, but her parents disapproved. Broadway plays were not opera, they said. If she was serious about singing, she should concentrate on her lessons. She agreed, and in the next two years increased her repertoire, or the roles that she could sing, to fifty operas. To her fluency in French and Italian she added a solid knowledge of German. Since most operas are sung in these three languages, it is necessary for singers to learn them.

During this period of intense study, she made her debut, or first opera appearance. In February of 1947 she played Frasquita, a gypsy, in *Carmen*. This *Carmen* was a Philadelphia Opera Company production, and the conductor was a friend of Miss Liebling. While performing in the opera, eager young Beverly kept her eyes and ears open. She learned the other roles and studied how the stars of the company performed them.

After the debut, she continued to look for opportunities to sing. There were few places to do this, making it a frustrating time for Beverly. The year she was nineteen, in order to keep performing, she toured colleges with four other students in a group called "The Estelle Liebling Singers."

A year later, she was offered a job singing in shipboard concerts on a South American cruise. At the time, her father was seriously ill, but the Silvermans had not told Beverly because they did not want to worry her. Beverly's parents thought she should take advantage of the opportunity the cruise presented, and urged her to accept the job. Mrs. Silverman saw her daughter off on the cruise, then returned home to take care of her husband.

While Beverly was on that cruise, her father died. His death was a great loss to the close family. Soon afterward, Beverly and her mother moved to a tiny apartment in Manhattan. Sydney and Stanley were both away at college; the two women were alone. Life was suddenly very different from old times in the house in Sea Gate.

Professionally, it was a quiet time, too. With no offers in opera, Beverly sang in a private club to support herself. At twenty-one, she had saved enough money from this job to take her mother to Europe. During the

Beverly at nineteen, the year that she toured colleges with the Estelle Liebling Singers.

trip, Beverly sang benefits aboard ship. When she arrived, she studied at the Paris Opera.

Restless and worried about her career when she finally returned home, Beverly talked with Miss Liebling, who contacted another old friend. Désiré Defrère, a stage director at the Metropolitan Opera, was directing a touring company, and accepted Beverly in the group.

This tour was a turning point in her career. Beverly, then only twenty-two years old, sang the leading role in *La Traviata*. In Guiseppe Verdi's opera, based on the novel *Camille*, two lovers are separated by the hero's father. After the heroine Violetta becomes ill, the lovers are reunited. But it is too late, and she dies in her lover's arms. Because of its appealing love story and melodic music, *La Traviata* is a great favorite among opera lovers. Violetta's romantic arias give a good singer a chance to show off her voice.

Defrère, confident that Beverly could be a successful opera singer, helped her believe in herself. Traveling by bus between cities, he reviewed each of her performances and made suggestions to improve her acting. He told her to read everything about each opera, studying the novels from which many opera stories are taken. In this way, she would learn how the original authors created their characters. Throughout her career, Beverly would follow his advice, gaining a deep understanding of the roles she performed.

A year later, she rejoined the touring company, this time in Georges Bizet's *Carmen*. The third year, however, she passed up a tour, feeling she had learned all she could from that kind of experience.

Once more, she looked for other opportunities. By now, she knew a few more people to call. Through one of them, she heard that the famous singer, Rosa Ponselle, was starting a new opera company in Baltimore, Maryland. Beverly tried for and won the title role in Jules Massenet's *Manon*. Her good reviews from that opera led to an audition with the San Francisco Opera Company. There, she made her debut as Helen of Troy in Arrigo Boito's *Mefistofele*. With the same company, she sang Donna Elvira in Wolfgang Mozart's *Don Giovanni*, as well as two other roles. The reviewers praised all of her performances. Singing with the San Francisco Opera, a solid, recognized company, made her name familiar. Slowly, she was building her reputation.

Each year, she added new performances to her repertoire, accepting offers from different parts of the country. By 1955, the year Beverly turned twenty-six, Miss Liebling decided that her student was ready to audition for the New York City Opera Company. The relatively new company, formed in 1944, was at the time no rival for the world-famed Metropolitan Opera. However, it had a permanent home at the City Center on Fifty-fifth Street in Manhattan and produced a full season of operas each fall.

Beverly made her debut with the New York City Opera in October, 1955 in Johann Strauss' *Die Fledermaus*. She quickly proved that she could step into new parts with little advance notice. The years of training with Miss Liebling, learning role after role, had prepared her well. In 1956 she appeared again with the company and then became a permanent member. Her dream had come true—she was an opera star at last.

At that time, City Opera performed in New York in the fall and then went on tour. Traveling with the company in Ohio in 1955, Beverly had met Peter Greenough, a newspaper editor, at a dinner party. He worked at the

One of Beverly's favorite roles throughout her career was Rosalinda in Die Fledermaus. *She made her debut in this opera.*

Cleveland Plain Dealer. Tall and attractive, with a friendly smile, Peter passed a matchbook down the table to Beverly. Inside, he had scrawled an invitation to have dinner with him the next evening.

Beverly had known and dated a number of men, but hadn't felt strongly about any of them. Yet after knowing Peter a short time, she was in love and sure that she wanted to marry him. At the time, however, he was already married, although he and his wife were separated and getting a divorce. A year later, Peter's divorce was final and he had gained custody of the couple's three daughters. Not long afterward, he and Beverly were married.

The wedding took place on November 17, 1956, in Estelle Liebling's studio. The couple exchanged their wedding vows standing in the center of the oriental rug, where Beverly first sang for Miss Liebling. It was a small, private ceremony attended only by the Silverman and Greenough families, Beverly's best friend, Sue Yager, the director Désiré Defrère, and of course, Miss Liebling.

After their honeymoon, Beverly and Peter returned to live in the Greenough house in Cleveland. Every few weeks, she traveled to different parts of the country for concerts that had been arranged a year earlier.

Meanwhile, the New York City Opera Company, then in serious financial trouble, hired conductor Julius Rudel as its artistic director. One of Rudel's first decisions was to add a spring season featuring modern American operas. As a result of his decision, the City Opera became the first showcase for American composers. People would now be able to see English-language operas on a more frequent basis.

In the first spring season, Beverly sang the title role

in Douglas Moore's *The Ballad of Baby Doe.* She became totally absorbed in the emotional story, almost living the part of Baby Doe. Excitement generated by its premier, or first performance, put the review on page one of the *New York Herald Tribune.*

At the close of the 1959 season, Beverly took a leave of absence to care for her new baby, Meredith "Muffy" Greenough, born on August 4 of that year. Peter had left the *Cleveland Plain Dealer* to become financial columnist for the *Boston Globe*, and the Greenoughs moved into a house in Milford, Massachusetts. Busy with the house and baby, Beverly nevertheless occasionally appeared as a guest artist.

On June 29, 1961, the Greenoughs' son, Peter, Jr., whom they nicknamed "Bucky," was born. Soon after his birth, Peter and Beverly suffered a double shock. Their daughter Muffy, although she seemed bright, had never spoken, even though she was two years old. One day Muffy got close to the hot stove, and Beverly thundered, "Hot! Hot!" The little girl repeated the word, the first she had ever spoken, over and over. Beverly and Peter then took Muffy for a hearing test; as feared, the test revealed that Muffy was deaf. Then, a month later, Bucky's doctor told them that the baby was mentally retarded.

For the next year, Beverly had almost no interest in her career. Friends tried to ease her pain, but they had little success. She repeatedly declined Julius Rudel's invitations to return to the City Opera. How could she go back to the difficult routine of the opera season when her children needed her, she thought. She stayed home, believing that only her efforts could change their lives.

Peter and Beverly had agreed that Muffy should be taught to speak instead of learning sign language. She attended a special school in Boston, but needed constant follow-up lessons at home. Both Muffy and her parents were patient with the long process of developing her speech. From the time the girl was very little, she was not allowed to have an object unless she asked for it. Pointing wasn't allowed.

In the meantime, caring for Bucky was becoming more and more difficult. A beautiful-looking child, he could do nothing for himself. Beverly's mother and Peter knew that Bucky would have to live at a special school for the retarded, but for years Beverly refused to accept this fact. She believed that if they loved him enough and only tried a little harder, they could keep him at home. As long as her children needed her, she would not leave them to resume her career.

Finally, Sarah Caldwell, the conductor, persuaded her to sing *Manon* with the Opera Company of Boston. The music from this story of a hopeless love affair is very sad. Beverly sang that night from the depths of her despair. The audience, sensing the genuine feeling in her performance, thundered its applause. Their reaction jolted her out of her sadness. For the first time in all those difficult months, she felt a renewal of spirit and energy. From that moment, she sought comfort and refuge in the music, no longer turning her pain inward, but freeing it in her singing.

A stern reminder from Julius Rudel of her contract with the City Opera brought her back to New York for a performance of *Baby Doe* in the spring of 1962. The following fall, she resumed her place as an active member of the company.

In 1966 the City Opera company was looking forward to moving uptown to the newly built Lincoln Center for the Performing Arts. For their very important opening there, Julius Rudel had chosen to do Georg Handel's *Julius Caesar*. He asked a former member of the company, then with the Metropolitan Opera, to come back to sing the lead role of Cleopatra.

Although she had never appeared in the opera, Beverly had sung a number of the arias in concerts. She was not only disappointed that she didn't get the part, but resented even more the suggestion that no one in the company could sing Cleopatra. Had the role gone to another company member, she would not have objected. The usually good-natured Beverly was angry. Convinced that as prima donna (the leading singer with the company) the part belonged to her, she demanded it. If she didn't get it, she told Julius Rudel, she would resign.

Rudel could not risk losing her. Beverly had her Cleopatra.

The Metropolitan Opera company, now City Opera's neighbor at Lincoln Center, had scheduled Samuel Barber's new opera *Antony and Cleopatra* for its premier in Lincoln Center. Why, everyone wondered, had Rudel chosen to pit his Cleopatra against the mighty Met's, played by Leontyne Price? The Lincoln Center "duel" had a surprise ending: Leontyne Price's singing was beautiful, but the Met production was too big, too lavish, too elaborate. Her singing got lost among all that. In contrast, the City Opera production featured simpler staging, which focused the attention on where it should be in an opera—the singing. At the end of the opening performance, Rudel, never free with compliments, exclaimed to Beverly, "You sang like a goddess tonight!"

Critics from all over the world, drawn to the Met opening, also attended City Opera's first night. Widely reviewed for the first time, Beverly earned their praises. Her voice had developed a new maturity. When she was younger, career goals were in her mind whenever she was onstage. After marriage and the birth of her children, her performances acquired a distinct new quality. The hardships of her handicapped children made her aware of other people's sufferings. She began to experience the healing capacity of music and its ability to bring joy. This sense of offering her voice as a gift enriched her performances.

"I think I became more aware of other people after my experience with my children," she said. "I began to listen to other people who were performing with me, which I'd never done before. You pay atention to other people when this kind of thing happens to you. Suddenly, you listen to what they're saying."

The Cleopatra role placed Beverly on center stage in the opera world. Offers to sing streamed in from Europe and South America. When Thomas Schippers, an American conductor living in Rome, needed to replace a soprano in Gioacchino Rossini's *The Siege of Corinth* at La Scala, he called Beverly. She left for Milan and had to learn the long and difficult role in four weeks.

Singing at La Scala was quite an experience. La Scala is considered by many opera lovers as the number-one opera house, and Italians regard their singers as highly as Americans do their ballplayers and popular entertainers. There, opera stars behave differently, too. The Italians expect a prima donna to create drama off-stage as well as on. In Milan, Beverly found that people paid little attention to her during rehearsals until she became angry. At home, her debut at La Scala put her on the cover of *Newsweek* magazine.

With Beverly's career in orbit, the Greenoughs moved from Milton, Massachusetts to an apartment in New York City. This new home became a jumping-off point for appearances all over the globe during the 1970s. Her repertoire was astonishing. She continued to add new roles to it, thoroughly studying each character as she had her earliest. Her dreams of fame and achievement had come true. One by one, she appeared on the great stages of the world, described years before by Estelle Liebling over those steaming cups of chocolate in the teacher's apartment.

The appearances, while thrilling to the girl from Brooklyn who had spent most of her career singing in the "other" New York opera company, made her appreciate the quality of that company. It was always good to come home to Lincoln Center to the solid New York City Opera productions.

"We [Americans] think European opera is better," she said. "Well, it's not! Our regional operas are far superior to regional operas in Europe. We have to get over the attitude that European singers are superior. We ought to be proud of our American singers."

In 1970 Beverly made her recital debut in New York City. Although she had sung in recitals, or concerts, in other cities, this was her first such appearance at home. Miss Liebling, too ill to attend, was with Beverly in spirit. The recital ended with a Portuguese folk song that Estelle had arranged for her student's tenth birthday present.

Miss Liebling died later that year; after that, Beverly ended all her recitals with the song, in memory of her teacher of thirty-four years. Estelle Liebling had been a long and faithful supporter, who left unforgettable memories with her student. Once, when she was ninety-one, she found fault with the way Beverly sang "The Jewel Song" from *Faust*. The next morning, her student received a phone call with the stern request to appear immediately for a practice session. In her will, Miss Liebling left Beverly the special cup in which she had served her hot chocolate when she was a little girl.

Between her travels, Beverly received a number of honors. President Richard Nixon appointed her to the Council on the National Endowment for the Arts and invited her to sing at the White House. She sang there again for President Gerald and Betty Ford and later, for President Jimmy and Rosalynn Carter. In 1974 Harvard University awarded her an honorary Doctor of Music degree. She accepted the degree as Mrs. Greenough, continuing a long tradition of Greenoughs with Harvard degrees. Beverly was honored for her "joyous personality, glorious voice, and deep knowledge of music and drama (that) bring delight to her audiences and distinction to her art."

Not until 1975 did she make her debut at the Metropolitan Opera House. A Met production of *The Siege of Corinth* reunited a number of musicians from Beverly's debut at La Scala six years earlier, including conductor Thomas Schippers. The excitement generated by two legends of American opera—the Met and Beverly Sills—filled newspapers and magazines for months before the event. On the evening of the performance, the plaza of Lincoln Center overflowed. Tremendous applause followed every aria. At the age of forty-six, Beverly had done it all, finally making it to the Met, known the world over as America's foremost opera house.

Beverly knew that, like all singers, her voice had a limited span of years. She was not going to hang on to the last notes when her voice was gone. When she no longer wanted to learn new roles, it would be time to stop. "I'll put my voice to bed and go quietly and with pride," she was quoted as saying.

That time came when she was fifty. Her official farewell at City Opera was without fanfare. In November 1979, she sang her last opera at the State Theater in a midweek performance of Gian Carlo Menotti's *La Loca*. It was one of her best performances in a difficult role. Modern operas are not kind to singers, but Beverly's voice was full and clear. Her curtain speech was brief. "Thank you for the marvelous love affair—the best is yet to be."

The real farewell came a year later in a star-studded fund-raising event. Beverly appeared in the second-act party scene of *Die Fledermaus* with celebrity friends. It was the opera in which she'd made her New York City Opera debut twenty-five years earlier.

But there was more to do. In 1980, at the age of fifty-one, she became director of the City Opera, taking over for her friend, Julius Rudel. Running the New York City Opera has never been easy. In a time when money for the arts is scarce, it is harder than ever. Although the job is demanding, Beverly's chances for success are good. Her skill in working with other people is a great asset in this job.

She wants to develop young singers and keep them at City Opera. Offering them good roles that they can't sing elsewhere is one way. That means choosing new productions with care. Her dream is to highlight City Opera as a showcase of American talent.

"She has a kind of magic," said her late friend and coach, Roland Gagnon. "She entrances people. She

Beverly's last regular performance was in La Loca *in 1979.*

changes things . . . . She's never impatient. It's her nature to be generous with people and they respond generously to her. She's a faithful friend and a perceptive one, who never loses her temper or her dignity. She knows how to compromise."

The magic that surrounds Beverly has made her an American institution. A proud prima donna onstage, offstage she is Bubbles, the tall redhead with the big grin who never forgets who she is. The exacting professional who began working for her dream in elementary school has enjoyed that dream's fulfillment. Her goal now is to help a new generation of singers find their dreams.

John Anderson.

WRITING MUSIC NEW AND OLD

RUTH CRAWFORD SEEGER: Her exploration of non-traditional, twentieth-century compositions and her compiling of years-old regional folk songs left Americans with a dual legacy.

Ruth Crawford Seeger always remembered July 3, 1907, her sixth birthday. She knew there was going to be a special surprise, but no one would tell her what it was. She had pleaded with her father for a hint, but he was firm. Besides, he told her, it was her mother's surprise. If her brother Carl knew, he wasn't telling, either.

When the last breakfast dish was put away, her mother took up a sewing basket and led her out to the front porch. There, she drew two chairs close together and showed Ruth how to mend socks. Feeling very grown-up, Ruth followed her mother's instructions. When she was able to get the darning thread twice across the hole in the heel of the sock, she smiled up at her mother. Was this the surprise, she wondered?

After lunch that day, Mrs. Crawford took off her apron, combed her own hair and Ruth's, and reached for her handbag. Ruth wondered aloud where they were going, but her mother wouldn't tell her. She only smiled and said, "You'll see!"

When they stopped at the house with the tubs of red and white geraniums out front, she looked at her mother, wide-eyed. Could this be where they were going? Ruth had never been in this house before, but she knew who lived here. On the way home from school, boys and girls carrying music books stopped here for their weekly piano lessons. Was she really old enough to start?

It seemed she was. Inside, she was introduced to the piano teacher who took out a big book and wrote Ruth's full name, Ruth Crawford, in large, flowing letters. The lessons could start next week, Mrs. Crawford was told. The teacher smiled at Ruth, saying that she looked like a very grown-up young lady who would practice every day. Ruth nodded her head. She was six; she was ready. The teacher told her how lucky she was to have a mother who was interested in music. Ruth was glad that the piano teacher knew her mother was smart.

On the way home, Clara Graves Crawford told her daughter how much she had wanted to learn piano when she was a little girl. But her father, Ruth's Grandfather Graves, who was a stern Methodist minister, had thought it a luxury. Only when Clara was sixteen years old and had left home to take a teaching job in Colorado, could she buy a pump organ for herself. Later, she worked in an office, and used some of the money she earned to buy the Sohmer piano that now stood in the Crawford's parlor. Clara was determined that her own daughter would begin lessons while she was still young.

Ruth was glad her father wasn't like Grandfather Graves. The Reverend Clark Crawford was kind and friendly to everyone. Every night after dinner he told Ruth a story. That night, for example, he made up a funny tale about the woman named Ruth in the Bible. As he was finishing, her mother began to play the "Bridal March" from Richard Wagner's opera *Lohengrin* on the piano. This music let the children know that it was time for bed. Ruth kissed her father and crossed his study, keeping time to the music. She hummed the tune as she passed through the hall and walked slowly up the stairs.

Because Mr. Crawford was frequently assigned to minister to different churches, his family moved many times. Ruth was born on July 3, 1901, while he was serving a church in East Liverpool, Ohio. In the next eleven years, the Crawfords moved to towns in Ohio, Missouri, and Indiana.

Ruth and her brother Carl made new friends wherever they went, but Ruth liked to be alone as well as with other children. When she was by herself, she could think about things she wanted to say or do. By the time she was seven, certain that she would be a poet, she began to fill notebooks with rhymes. Reading also became important to her. She wished that people would start giving her books for presents, instead of toys. Lucky Carl, at twelve, was too old for toys and he got books!

In 1911 the Crawfords moved to Jacksonville, Florida. A bright youngster, Ruth had skipped several grades during elementary school. Now she found herself in classes with older students. They all seemed to be talking about which boys and girls liked each other. Not ready for that, she began to spend more time with books and her piano.

When Ruth was thirteen, her father, who had not been well for a long time, died. Mrs. Crawford had to support the two children and herself. They had to leave the church house for the new minister. Clara Crawford rented a large house and took in roomers, people who lived alone and didn't need much space. The money they paid for their rooms helped the family meet its needs.

In high school in Jacksonville, Ruth felt lonely. The few friends she made were like herself, preferring books and music to parties. Carl's friends, who kept busy planning dances and trips to the beach, called her a bookworm. But Ruth didn't mind.

She knew that she had ideas to express. What form they would take, she wasn't sure. Sometimes she felt herself pulled in two different directions. After school, she practiced the piano for hours. In study hall at school, she continued to compose rhymes in her notebook. For some time she had been writing a major poem. When she finally stopped working on it, she found that it contained eight hundred two-line rhymes!

When the United States entered World War I, Carl left to join the army. One by one, his friends went off, too. In her diary, Ruth wrote about her fears for them and for everyone suffering in the war. When she thought about the war, her own problems with growing up seemed small and foolish.

After she graduated from high school, Ruth looked for a way to support herself with her music. Luckily she was able to find two jobs in which she could use her training. In one of them, she taught piano at the School of Musical Art in Jacksonville. For the other, she was in charge of the music program at a nearby kindergarten.

When she was not at work, she was composing

music. Ruth saved her money, intent on leaving Jacksonville to study music in a large city. Her only luxury was attending concerts of visiting artists: pianists Percy Aldridge Grainger, Josef Hoffman, and the great Ignace Paderewski.

In the fall of 1920, at the age of nineteen, Ruth left Jacksonville to study at the American Conservatory of Music in Chicago. She had enough money to last one year if she was careful.

Excited by the city and the conservatory, she nevertheless missed her family. In letters home, she described her piano study with Heniot Lévy and harmony lessons with Jon Palmer and Adolf Weidig.

When she wasn't studying or practicing, Ruth explored Chicago, visiting the Opera House each week during the season and attending concerts at Orchestra Hall. Like other students, she accepted free tickets and bought standing room places or the cheapest seats high in the balconies. New friends among the faculty and students at the conservatory eased the pangs of homesickness.

Later in the year, with Louise Robyn, she studied music and materials for teaching children, and began to observe children's music classes. At the end of the school year, Ruth was awarded a teacher's certificate from the American Conservatory. Her savings were gone, but she went home to Jacksonville determined to return to the conservatory for more study. Looking back on the first year, she was pleased with her progress. She wanted to learn more about music theory.

Back in Chicago the following year, she took a job as a coat checker at a theater in the "loop," or downtown section of the city. The pay was not much, but she was

Ruth during her years at the American Conservatory in Chicago.

able to study during the shows. When the plays were worthwhile, she watched them. Students working at other theaters often exchanged places with her, making it possible to see a number of good plays.

During her first year at the conservatory, Ruth had begun to suffer from tense muscles during piano practice. The problem continued into the second year, interfering with her growth as a performer. Her work in theory was completely satisfying to her, however, and she began to compose music of her own that won Adolf Weidig's praise. During that second year, her interest gradually shifted from performing to composing.

To add to the small income from her theater job, Ruth instructed private piano students. Supporting herself in this way during her second and third years at the conservatory, she earned her Bachelor of Music degree in 1923.

After graduation she stayed in Chicago, teaching private piano and theory lessons. The following fall, her mother came to live with her in a small, rented apartment. Mrs. Crawford, who loved music and played the piano well herself, was delighted with her daughter's accomplishments.

A year after she received her bachelor's degree, Ruth joined the staff of the American Conservatory, teaching piano and music theory while working toward her master's degree. Her work continued to be influenced by Adolf Weidig, the associate director of the school. A composer himself, whose work was considered somewhat conservative by other modern musicians, he encouraged his students to explore new directions. He allowed Ruth the freedom to develop her own style of composition.

While continuing her graduate studies and her teaching at the conservatory, Ruth began teaching at Elmhurst College, near Chicago, in 1926. Her studies went beyond the classroom and studio. For part of one season, she played the triangle in the civic orchestra. Surrounded by other instruments, she heard the music in a different way than she did as a member of the audience.

In 1924 and 1925, she composed five preludes for piano. These short pieces, written for her own instrument, contain elements of style that occur in her later, more mature work. They were followed by a second group, Piano Preludes 6 through 10. Prelude 6 in this group she dedicated to Djane Lavoie-Herz, her piano teacher for four years.

Madame Herz played an important role in Ruth's artistic development. Her studio on the north side of Chicago was a gathering place for composers and performers who were interested in trying out new musical forms and ideas. For centuries, music had been composed according to certain tones, or sounds, arranged in definite patterns called scales. Each piece of music composed in these scales had a single tone that became more important than the other tones and was called the key tone. Thus, music might be in the key of C or another note. As time passed, changes occurred in the development of music, but most of the changes were gradual. Songs were written for more than one voice; the small group of stringed instruments grew to include all the different sounds of a symphony orchestra. With these developments, however, composers continued to follow the traditional ways.

By the early twentieth century, a number of composers believed that the established forms of music had been taken as far as they could. These composers broke away from the traditional arrangement of tones and scales. When they did, they created new sounds arranged in unfamiliar patterns.

Amazed listeners, accustomed to the old patterns, often rejected the new music. Nevertheless, many composers continued to experiment. In addition, they met at places like Madame Herz's studio to share ideas and to encourage each other.

Talking with other musicians at Madame Herz's helped Ruth to refine her own ideas. A Russian pianist and composer, Alexander Scriabin, whose style she studied, influenced her work. She also met Henry Cowell, who understood what she was groping toward in her student compositions. A composer himself, Cowell seemed to know everyone connected with the new music. He helped arrange performances that introduced modern compositions to a wider audience. With his help, Ruth published her Piano Preludes 6, 7, 8, and 9 in the yearly publication, *New Music*, in 1927. Two years earlier, her first solos, Preludes 1 through 5, had been performed in New York City's Town Hall. Her work was becoming known outside the small circle of experimental musicians in Chicago.

A friend recommended her to the poet Carl Sandburg, who needed a piano teacher for his children. Each week, Ruth went to the white frame house in Elmhurst, not far from the college where she was teaching. The association with Sandburg was another milestone in her development as an artist. She wrote the piano arrangements for several songs in his *American Songbag*, published in 1927. Ruth also wrote music of her own for several of Sandburg's poems. Five of her songs were composed before 1929 and another three shortly afterward. All eight songs, which highlight the words in Sandburg's verse, reflect Ruth's own enthusiasm for reading and writing poetry.

Mrs. Crawford, who had lived just long enough to enjoy her daughter's early successes, died in 1928. Ruth missed her mother. She had been a good friend and companion, listening to Ruth's compositions and encouraging her in her work.

The following year, Ruth received her Master of Music degree from the conservatory *cum laude*, meaning "with honors." That summer, she accepted a fellowship at

Ruth with Carl Sandburg, whose poems she set to music.

the MacDowell Colony in Peterboro, New Hampshire, and did not return to Chicago. The MacDowell Colony is a retreat, a private, secluded home where qualified writers, artists, and composers can work without the distractions of everyday life.

From New Hampshire, Ruth went to New York to stay at the apartment of Blanche Walton, a music patron and friend of composer Henry Cowell. Cowell and Mrs. Walton were anxious to have Ruth take private lessons with composer Charles Seeger. He was an authority on the new music, and they were certain he could help Ruth.

Charles Seeger's musical background was rich and varied. As a young composer, he had gone to Europe after his graduation from Harvard University in 1908. During the 1910-1911 music season, he conducted the orchestra of the Cologne Opera in Germany. Unfortunately, a hearing loss ended his hopes for a conducting career. Instead, he continued to compose and began to study the relation between music and society. From 1912 to 1919, he was chair of the music department at the University of California in Berkeley. There he developed the first courses in musicology, a study of the science, history, forms, and methods of music. Most of his compositions, which he left at Berkeley when he came to New York, were destroyed in a fire there in 1926.

In 1921, Charles became a lecturer and instructor at the Institute of Musical Art in New York City, which later became the Juilliard School. Later he joined the faculty of the New School for Social Research. There, with Henry Cowell, he taught the first courses in ethnomusicology, which is the study of the music of different cultures. At the same time, Charles wrote music reviews for several newspapers and journals, including *The Daily Worker*, a Communist newspaper, where he wrote under the pen name Carl Sand.

Seeger was cool to the idea of women composing music, however, and he had no interest in meeting Ruth. Even when Cowell showed him some of her work, he was unimpressed. Nevertheless, at his friend's insistence that "this woman is different," he agreed to give her a try.

Ruth herself was curious about Seeger. Aware of his disdain for women composers, she also knew his reputation as a great teacher. She decided to let her work speak for itself and went to meet him. Seeger, a tall, handsome man who wore glasses and a moustache, looked very much like a professor. Although he had not expected to find her work worthwhile, he soon realized that Ruth had real talent. Henry Cowell was right. This woman *was* different!

Meeting Seeger was another turning point in Ruth's musical development. She came to agree with her new teacher that in order to break the rules of composition the composer must be ready to substitute new and equally genuine rules. As a result of her study with Seeger, her work acquired a strong sense of organization.

In 1930, she completed her *Piano Study in Mixed Accents*, which showed a Seeger influence, followed by four "*Diaphonic*" *Suites* for wind and string instruments. In that same year, she composed "Rat Riddles," the first of *Three Songs* that she completed in 1932. This work, based on Sandburg's poems, was chosen to represent the United States at the Festival of the International Society for Contemporary Music held in Amsterdam in 1933. Later, *Three Songs* was published in the annual edition of *New Music*.

Ruth's compositions won her a Guggenheim fellowship, the first awarded to a woman. In June 1930 she sailed to Europe, free to study as she chose, with no need to worry about money. While there, she wrote *Chants for Women's Chorus*, her *String Quartet*, and "In Tall Grass," the second song of the Sandburg series, *Three Songs*. The string quartet is Ruth's best-known work.

Returning to New York in 1931, she married Charles Seeger. Fifteen years older than Ruth, Charles had been married before and was the father of three sons: Charles, John, and Peter. After their marriage, Ruth continued to work on her music, completing "Prayers of Steel," the last part of the Sandburg series.

In 1933 Henry Cowell introduced Ruth and Charles to the Composers Collective, a group of New Yorkers who were trying to link music with social issues. The United States was enduring the Great Depression, a time of economic hardship. With millions of people out of work, poverty and hunger were widespread. The collective's members hoped to express the people's suffering in their music. Ruth wrote two songs for the group, "Sacco, Vanzetti," a song of protest about a famous trial, and "Chinaman, Laundryman."

Working with the collective prompted the Seegers to question their own musical education. They realized how little they knew about American folk music, the songs of the countryside that were seldom heard in the cities. As they learned more about folk songs, they were surprised to find in them elements of the new music. As a result, they began to wonder if the division that people made between music composed for symphony orchestras and that for folk instruments really did exist.

On August 15, 1933, Ruth and Charles had their first baby, Michael. After their second child Peggy was born, less than two years later, the family moved to the Washington, D.C. area. Charles had accepted a job in Washington—he was to be an advisor in music with the Resettlement Administration of the United States government.

Soon after their move, the Seegers visited the Archives of the Library of Congress where a man named John Lomax had been depositing records of folk music. With his son Alan, Lomax had traveled to prisons and farm areas throughout the United States, listening to and recording the songs of the people they met.

In the mid-1930s, only a few dozen folk songs were well known outside the regions in which they had developed. The Lomaxes had published a book that Charles Seeger hoped would introduce the songs to a wider audience. By then, he and Ruth viewed folk music as part of a

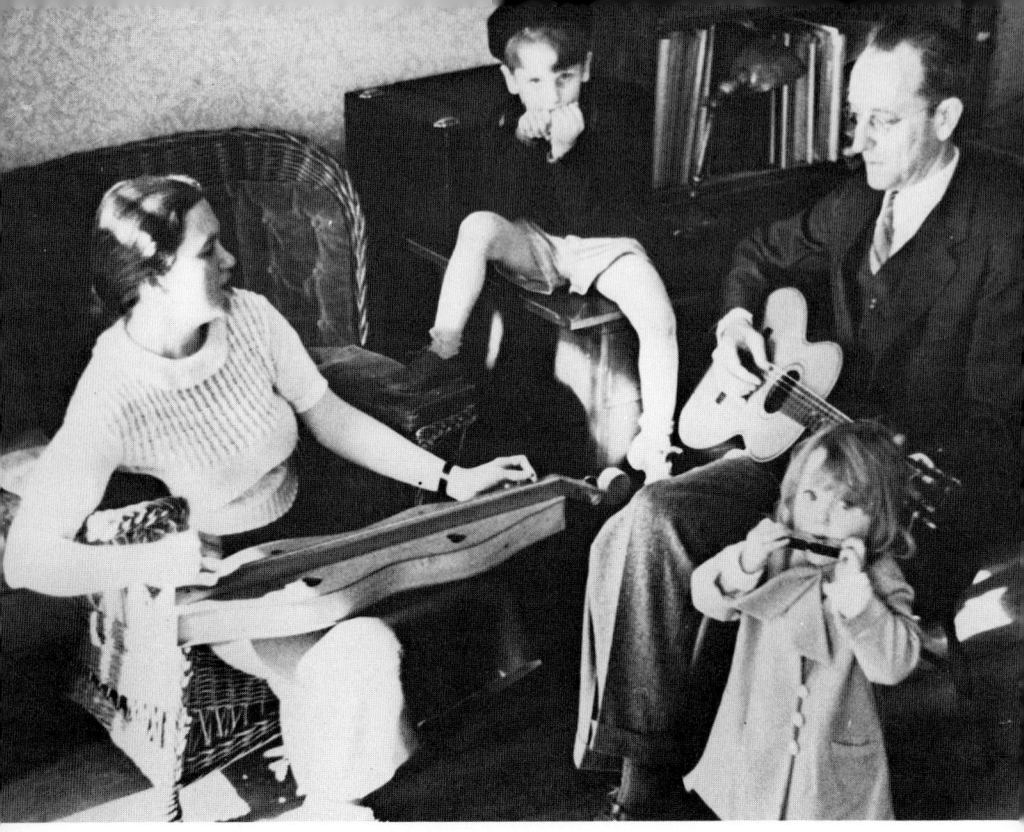

Ruth and Charles Seeger lived in a house full of music. Here they sing and play with Michael and Peggy.

process in which ordinary people could express their true feelings.

From copies of the records in the American Folk Music Archive, Ruth listened to and transcribed, or wrote down, the notes, so that the songs could be read and played. The work was fascinating but demanding. Although some of the recordings had been made in studios, many were recorded in places where the Lomaxes found singers—barns, prison cells, meeting halls, and out of doors.

Closeted in an upstairs bedroom with a record player and earphones, Ruth listened carefully to each aluminum record, trying to write the music exactly as she heard it. Sometimes, if a singer slurred a note, or if background noises interfered, the task was much more difficult and she asked for help. Peter Seeger remembers his stepmother pacing about for hours, replaying a tiny section of one record, asking everyone who came in what they thought a particular note was. At times Ruth argued fiercely with Alan Lomax over the music, he remembering the singer, and she insisting that the record was different.

During the next few years, she transcribed the music for hundreds of records from the Archive. Some of this work appeared in the Lomaxes' book, *Our Singing Country*, published in 1941. In her introduction to the book, Ruth suggested tempos and singing styles for people unfamiliar with folk songs. She advised against fancy endings, preferring to close a song simply, the way a folk singer would. For the Lomaxes' later book, *Folk Songs, U.S.A.*, which contained one hundred eleven songs, Ruth and Charles wrote the piano accompaniments and a musical foreword.

After the Seegers moved to Washington, two more children were born: Barbara, in 1937, and Penny, in 1943. Caring for six children was a difficult task, but Ruth's energy seemed boundless. After Mike and Peggy began going to school all day and Barbara was in nursery school, her work took a new direction. In addition to editing the folk song collections and giving private piano lessons, she directed the music program at one nursery school and taught music at three others.

The family helped Ruth reproduce a book of folk songs for children that she made for Barbara's nursery school. Mike and Peggy glued together the copies of each page and put them into looseleaf binders. Several years later, a book company published it as Ruth's first collection, *American Folk Songs for Children.*

In 1941, the same year that the Lomax book was published, Charles was appointed chief of the music division of the Pan American Union. The appointment introduced the Seegers to the folk music of Central and South America. Ruth edited the music in *Folk Songs of the Dominican Republic*, published in 1955.

During the years of her music research, Ruth did no composing. Not until 1941 did she return to her own music. In "Rissolty Rossolty," a work for a small orchestra commissioned by CBS for its program, "School of the Air," she displayed her rich background of folk music. Using the tunes of three old songs, "Rissolty Rossolty" seems simple and charming on the surface. Yet it is made up of several complex musical patterns and is equal to the best compositions produced by other musicians of the period.

Despite the demands of her active family, Ruth continued to teach and edit. The Seeger children, including Charles's son Pete, shared the family interest in folk music, studying and performing. Soon after the birth of Penny, the family moved to a three-story house in Chevy Chase, Maryland.

One day, when Peggy was lost in a busy department store in downtown Washington, D.C., she was found by a friendly store clerk, Elizabeth Cotten. Elizabeth told Ruth that she was looking for a housekeeping job. Ruth liked the warm, southern woman and offered her a job. In time, Elizabeth became a second mother to Barbara and Penny, who called her Libba. After she had been with the Seegers for several years, she began to sing and play the banjo and guitar for them. One of the songs she sang was

Ruth published several books of folk songs for children. These nursery-school children are learning one of the songs from her.

"Freight Train," which she had written at the age of twelve. The whole family marveled at the way Elizabeth played the instruments—upside down and backwards with her left hand!

Five years after Penny was born, Ruth's first book, the original family-bound *American Folk Songs for Children,* was printed and published by a book company. It was followed by *Animal Folk Songs for Children* in 1950. Two other collections, *Christmas Folk Songs for Chil-*

dren and *Let's Build a Railroad,* would later be published.

Through those busy days, the five-foot, two-inch tall woman moved swiftly, her cheeks rosy and her black eyes sparkling. Her long dark braids were crossed on top of her head, needing no attention all day. Clothes were chosen for ease of care and wearing. Every minute counted. She stopped only to drink endless cups of coffee that were kept warming in a pot on the kitchen stove, to kiss a scraped knee, or to settle a dispute between the children.

Libba and other housekeepers took good care of the children, and did the work of the large household. But Ruth was always there at home, within call when help was needed or a question had to be answered. She maintained her fast pace until dinnertime, when the family sat down together and shared the activities of the day with one another. After dinner, there was time for performing: Peggy played the piano and guitar and Mike the autoharp, while Barbara and Penny sang. Charles liked to sing Spanish songs with Peggy, including a favorite, "Adelita." Sometimes Ruth went back to the piano to play the children to sleep.

Despite her many responsibilities, Ruth completed her *Wind Quintet* in 1952. A return to her earlier style, the composition had a little of the informal feeling of "Rissolty Rossolty." It contained elements of modern music that were by then familiar to concert audiences.

This composition was Ruth's last work. In the summer of 1953, after an operation, she began a series of X-ray treatments for cancer. Hoping that they would be successful, she tried to continue her regular schedule. But gradually she grew weaker.

On Wednesday, November 18, 1953, Ruth was supposed to appear at the *Washington Post* Children's Book Fair where her books were to be featured. Too ill to attend, she asked Michael and Peggy to go. In her place, they played banjo and guitar and sang songs from the collections. At noon on that day, Ruth, who was fifty-two years old, died at home.

Despite her early death, Ruth made two significant contributions to American music. First, her experiments in form and expression helped musicians and concert-goers alike to develop an appreciation for modern music. Indeed, many experts believe that she would have become one of the most famous composers of twentieth-century music if she had lived longer. Second, Ruth played a very important role in acquainting millions of Americans with their national music. The countless hours she spent transcribing songs and editing music books is one of the reasons Americans have such a rich heritage of folk music.

Most people are unaware of Ruth's achievements, because she did not live long enough to continue her work. Those who know her 1931 *String Quartet* appreciate the quality of her original music. Americans honor her memory, though, each time they sing or listen to one of the folk tunes she thought it was important for them to get to know.

By 1950, folk tunes from the Eastern hills and hollows, from across the plains and deserts, and down from the Western mountains hummed in the rhythms of American life. The love of that music, kindled in the Seeger household, now flames in the cities and countryside of America and England. Strumming their instruments, the Seegers continue to lead the singing.

MAKING A JOYFUL NOISE

LEONTYNE PRICE: This prima donna's earliest successes—as a concert and recital singer, as the inspiration to great composers, and as a Broadway star—were crowned by a long, acclaimed career and performances at the great opera houses of the world.

Katie Price's high, clear voice had a special lift as she sang with the choir of St. Paul's Methodist Church on a Sunday morning in 1927. Joyfully, she raised her voice to heaven, celebrating once again the gift of life within her. Married thirteen years, Katie and James Price had almost given up the hope of having children. Now, Katie was almost ready to give birth to their first child.

Mary Leontine Price, who would someday be known as Leontyne Price, was born on the following Thursday, February 10, 1927. Years later, Katie Price would say that her daughter's beautiful voice sprang from her joy that Sunday morning in church.

From the beginning, Leontyne was surrounded by music. Her father played baritone horn in parades and special events with the Laurel Eagle Band. Her mother loved singing with her church's choir. As soon as Leontyne was old enough, she went with her mother to choir practice.

By the time she was three and a half, Leontyne was tapping out tunes on a toy piano and singing for her mother. A year later she began private lessons with piano teacher Mrs. Hattie McInnis. By then the Prices had another child, George, born two years after Leontyne. Both brother and sister would later credit their parents' can-do attitude and encouragement to achieve as the sturdy base of their lives.

Laurel, Mississippi, where the Price family lived, was an industrial town; a sawmill was one of the chief businesses there. As a teenager, James Price had come to Laurel to work in the lumber company and help support his family. He learned carpentry and plumbing and later became a skilled carriage operator at the mill, guiding logs as they were cut into boards.

Katie Baker was living in Laurel with her married sister Evelina Greer. Katie had wanted to be a registered nurse, but her parents had been unable to send her to school for the training. Katie then did the next best thing: she became a practical nurse and midwife, helping other women bring their children into the world.

When James and Katie met, they knew that they fit together. They were married in Evelina and Buddy Greer's house. The Prices were determined to give their children, when they came, every opportunity to learn, grow, and experience life.

Both parents worked hard to provide a good home for Leontyne and George. Although there was little extra money, the children had music lessons. When she didn't have cash for Hattie McInnis, Mrs. Price ironed the piano teacher's clothes. The children were expected to study hard and practice their lessons. Each one had chores in addition to music practice. Their parents often said to them, "Be the best at whatever it is you decide to be, and we will be proud of you. We don't care if it's washing dishes or digging ditches—be the best."

As Leontyne said later, "I had a happy childhood. I was poor, but I had enough to eat and I had enough clothes to wear. I liked the world I had as a child. The main thing is there was so much love inside the home I was raised in. My brother and I were very close. My parents were not the kind of people who were afraid to show us they were proud of us, and I think that has been a very good thing for me. . . .If there were problems, and I think there must have been many, they were settled calmly. I never heard my parents argue with one another. I always saw my father treat my mother with the greatest respect. . . .We had a nice time as children."

Laurel was unusual for a town in the South at that time: although black and white children attended separate schools, the neighborhoods had people of both races living in them. Employees of the lumber companies and other plants lived close to their workplaces. James and Katie taught the children to judge people as individuals, not by skin color. That was their way and the way in the town.

Across town, Leontyne's Aunt Evelina and Uncle Buddy Greer lived in a house on property belonging to the Alexander Chisholms, a white family for whom the Greers worked. Evelina was a maid in the Chisholm house and prepared meals on the cook's night out. Buddy did the yard work.

When she was old enough to cross town, Leontyne went to visit her aunt and uncle and came to know the Chisholm family. Mr. and Mrs. Chisholm believed in equality, and used their wealth to help other people; the Chisholm family supported a scholarship program for black students. The Chisholms were to become friends and supporters of Leontyne. Elizabeth Chisholm in particular encouraged Leontyne's musical talent.

At ten years old Leontyne began playing the piano at Sunday school. She sang with both the church and school choirs, and was soon singing and playing solo at club meetings, benefits, and parties. In high school, Leontyne, with her lovely soprano voice, began to sing at parties in the Chisholm house. Before long, other invitations followed, and soon she was singing for many local weddings as well as funerals. "Because" was the favorite wedding song and "Homing" the usual choice for funerals. She sang these with such feeling that, at one funeral, the grief-stricken family asked her to stop. Angrily, Leontyne vowed, "That's the last funeral I'll ever do." And it was.

At Oak Park Vocational High School, where four years of music appreciation was required of everyone, Leontyne joined the choral group, which won competitions at both district and state levels. Mrs. Hattie McInnis, her long-time teacher, directed the chorus, and asked Leontyne to play for concerts. In high school, like her friends, Leontyne went to movies and dances, and even became a cheerleader. Despite a busy schedule of church, school, and music activities, she also did very well in her studies.

One Sunday, Mr. and Mrs. Price invited the guest minister from their church, an army chaplain from nearby Camp Shelby, to their home for dinner. As she always did after dinner, Leontyne played the piano and sang. When the chaplain had listened for half an hour, he asked, "How would you like a scholarship to Wilberforce College in Ohio?" It was almost too good to be true! Leontyne had been planning to attend a local Mississippi college until the chaplain arranged for her scholarship. She enrolled in the College of Education and Industrial Arts in Wilberforce. (The university was later renamed Central State.) Leontyne had plans of becoming a music teacher and of helping George once he was in college. In 1944, feeling very grown up, she left for college in Ohio with her first piece of luggage and two coats.

As a member of the college glee club, she traveled to concerts throughout the state, and to Chicago and Pittsburgh. Her voice attracted attention from college president Charles H. Wesley, who frequently asked her to sing for visiting officials. In her black dress, Leontyne sang "Homing" for the Ohio Board of Education and other groups.

Meanwhile, her brother George won a full athletic scholarship to South Carolina State College. He would not need her help to pay for college. Leontyne was free to dream a little. Maybe she could take a chance on trying to become a performer rather than a teacher, she thought.

Putting Leontyne through college was something of a hardship for her parents. During the summer of her junior year in school, Mr. and Mrs. Chisholm went to visit James Price. They wanted Leontyne to have the opportunity to develop her voice, and they knew it would cost a great deal of money—more than James Price could afford. Realizing the Mr. Price was a proud and sensitive man, the Chisholms had come to ask his permission to help Leontyne. James Price agreed.

Leontyne's dream was becoming a little clearer. She was awarded a Bachelor of Arts degree from Central State College in 1948. With the encouragement of Dr. Wesley, she applied for and won a scholarship to the Juilliard School of Music in New York City. That same year, Paul Robeson, the famous black singer, heard her perform at a concert in Antioch, Ohio. Impressed with her voice, Robeson sang in a benefit concert that raised $1,000 for Leontyne's Juilliard expenses. The Chisholms would also be helping her with money. Leontyne was grateful, not only for these gifts, but for the way the Chisholms had offered it to her father.

At Juilliard, Leontyne's voice teacher, Florence Page Kimball, did not notice anything unusual about her new student. To Kimball, Leontyne was a shy but pleasant young woman with a reasonably good voice. Among the Juilliard students, who had been selected from the best young musicians in the United States and abroad, she did not seem outstanding at first.

During the time she studied at Juilliard, Leontyne took part in every available musical activity. She sang at the traditional Sunday night candlelight suppers in the lobby of the International House, where she lived with other out-of-town Juilliard students. She also performed in several student music productions.

After seeing her first opera, Ferruccio Busoni's *Turandot*, at the City Center, her dream began to focus, and she tried out for Juilliard's Opera Workshop. She was admitted in her second year at the school, a year earlier than most students.

Hearing her sing the "Lament" from Henry Purcell's *Dido and Aeneas*, in his "Introduction to Opera" course, Frederic Cohen, the workshop director, told his wife,

"We have the voice of the century." About this student he had no doubts. This young soprano would be famous one day, he was sure.

Still, Leontyne fretted that her progress was too slow. She longed to have something to look forward to, a sign that one day she would be successful. Almost as soon as she confessed to a friend that she was losing hope, she learned that she had won an important role in a workshop production of Guiseppe Verdi's opera *Falstaff.*

When Leontyne played the part of Mistress Ford, Florence Kimball heard a new quality in her student's voice. The young woman from Laurel was the outstanding singer in the opera. As it happened, composer Virgil Thompson attended the *Falstaff* production, and he agreed with Kimball. He knew he'd found the perfect person to play Saint Cecilia in the revival, or restaging, of his opera *Four Saints in Three Acts.* He was planning on opening this production in 1952 in Paris.

Leontyne was on her way to fame. Leaving Juilliard to accept her first professional assignment, she nevertheless continued studying with Florence Kimball. While Leontyne was appearing in the Thompson work, she sang for Robert Breen, director and co-producer of a new production of *Porgy and Bess,* the George Gershwin musical. Her singing of "Summertime" from the show convinced him that she could play the role of Bess, and he immediately offered her the part. Also in a title role was the popular baritone William Warfield, who had appeared on Broadway in the musical *Call Me Mister* and in the movie version of *Showboat.*

The Dallas opening performance of *Porgy and Bess* in June 1952 brought family and old friends together. Leontyne's brother George was an army lieutenant then,

The experience Leontyne got in recitals and concerts, while starring on Broadway, and on NBC Opera Theater helped prepare her for her opera stage debut in Dialogues of the Carmelites *in 1957.*

on leave after being wounded in Korea. He sat with the Chisholms and other friends from Laurel.

The new production was a hit. In the *Saturday Review*, critic John Rosenfield praised Leontyne's bright, clear voice and exciting acting. *Porgy and Bess* began a long cross-country tour.

Almost from their first meeting, Leontyne and Bill Warfield were attracted to each other. By the time the show opened in Dallas, they knew they were in love. After the tour's last performance, in Washington, D.C., Leontyne and Bill hired a bus to drive the entire company to New York City. There they were married at Bill's church, the Abyssinian Baptist Church, on August 31, 1952. Six cast members were bridesmaids, and one of the Chisholm daughters represented Laurel at the wedding. At the reception afterward in Harlem's Hotel Teresa, the newlyweds cut a wedding cake decorated with the opening bars of Porgy's song, "Bess, You Is My Woman Now," from the show.

Following the ceremony, the wedding party returned to Washington, where the cast was scheduled to leave the next day on a U.S. government plane bound for Berlin. The government was sponsoring a European tour of *Porgy and Bess*, with performances in London, Paris, and Vienna. When this tour ended the following February, the show opened a ten-month run at the Ziegfeld Theater on Broadway. William Warfield, who had other contracts to honor, did not appear in this Broadway production.

Leontyne continued playing the role of Bess, taking time off to fulfill her own concert engagements. She became what she later called "the contemporary composer's Girl Friday," singing the music of Igor Stravinsky, Samuel Barber, and Henri Sauguet in concert. The light musical role of Bess had not made her forget her primary goal of singing serious music.

While composing his "Hermit Songs," Samuel Barber heard Leontyne sing; her voice became a major influence on the songs. In October 1953, she sang them in a special concert at the Library of Congress in Washington, D.C. She repeated the performance in Rome and later in New York City's Town Hall. At her Town Hall debut, the *New York Herald Tribune* reviewer said he heard a "goddess performing among us."

Leontyne's presence on Broadway, combined with her concert appearances, attracted the attention of some important people. By the time she left the cast of *Porgy and Bess* in 1954, her concert career looked promising.

At that time, television, just becoming widespread, was changing American opera. It introduced these classics to millions of people who lived far from big city stages. In the mid-1950s, "NBC Opera Theater" broadcast a series of operas written in or translated into English. Its producers, who signed up well-known singers for leading roles, also were on the lookout for new talent.

Long after Herman Peter Adler, NBC Opera Theater's musical director, had seen *Porgy and Bess*, Leontyne's vivid acting and lovely voice remained in his memory. When an English-language version of Giacomo Puccini's *Tosca* was chosen for NBC's 1955 season, Adler thought of Leontyne.

For the leading role he would need a singer with an unusually large range, one whose voice could show contrasting feelings by moving from the lowest notes to the highest easily. In the opera, Floria Tosca, a gentle, loving young singer, kills the evil Baron Scarpio in order to save her lover. As Tosca turns her rage on Scarpio, the singer's voice must keep pace with the action and emotions.

At the end of her interview with Adler and producer Samuel Chotzinoff, Leontyne left in a cloud, feeling she was close to a breakthrough in her career. Chotzinoff wanted to hire her immediately; both men knew she would be vocally perfect for the role. However, there was a potential problem, they thought, if they decided to cast Leontyne as Tosca.

Although the spotlight of public attention had not yet been turned on it fully, a great deal of racial prejudice existed in the 1950s. Black people were extremely aware of the unfair treatment they received, but it would take the growing civil rights movement to bring prejudice to everyone's attention. Leontyne's experience at Juilliard, where she was accepted for her ability, only confirmed what her family believed—that people should concentrate on each individual's worth and try to ignore racial differences. However, on the *Porgy and Bess* tour, Leontyne had received a crash course in surviving America's prejudice against its own citizens. Special transportation, eating, and housing arrangements had to be made for the cast, for in many places blacks were not allowed to use the same facilities as whites.

Leontyne was cast as Tosca despite any problems the producers thought they might have. She knew how unusual it was for a black singer to be offered a leading role. While preparing for *Tosca*, however, she did not know about the objections and protests her appearance was creating among out-of-town broadcasters. Concentrating on her preparations, she put everything else out of her mind. Adler and his associates, wanting her to give her best performance, did not discuss this with her.

Afterward, when she learned about the stir the production had created, she shrugged off the news. The singer was satisfied that she'd given a first-class performance, and that was what really mattered. "We created a rumpus, but it was a successful rumpus," she laughed.

Leontyne's appearance as Tosca, a role in which she wore no white makeup to disguise her race, was a major breakthrough in the struggle against prejudice. For her, it was an unusual debut, or first appearance, in grand opera. Unlike other singers chosen by NBC for principal roles, she had not yet appeared in person on an opera stage.

Because of her performance, NBC offered her a contract to sing in Wolfgang Mozart's *The Magic Flute.* In 1956 she sang the role of Donna Anna in Mozart's *Don Giovanni.* The popular Sunday afternoon series, broadcast to millions, was her training ground for live opera. She learned a great deal from director Peter Herman Adler and, long after the broadcasts, continued to ask his advice.

Also in 1956, she sang Cleopatra in a concert performance of Georg Handel's *Julius Caesar.* With the American National Theatre Academy (ANTA) she visited India on an American State Department tour.

Almost overnight, she had become a celebrity. *Mademoiselle* magazine placed her on its 1955 list of outstanding women. Before she ever appeared on a professional opera stage, the TV broadcasts had established Leontyne as an American opera star.

She didn't have long to wait for her stage debut, however. The San Francisco Opera Company invited her to join the first American performance of composer Fran-

Leontyne as Tosca in a Metropolitan Opera production of Tosca, *a role she first performed on television.*

cis Poulenc's *Dialogues of the Carmelites*. Poulenc, impressed after hearing Leontyne on the concert stage, was excited about her singing the role of the Mother Superior in his new opera at its American premier.

On the night of Leontyne's first appearance with the San Francisco Opera, September 20, 1957, she admitted to what she called "a cold petrification," or trembling with fear. Despite all her concert experience and the TV broadcasts, Leontyne knew her stage debut was different. In the audience were reviewers who judge opera singers by their performances as part of the whole production. Between her and that audience, no safety net existed. But Leontyne did not disappoint them; she lived up to the promise of her TV and concert appearances.

A month later, during the intermission, or time between acts, of her third performance of the *Dialogues*, the opera company's manager came to her dressing room. He told her that Antoinette Stella, currently starring in Verdi's opera *Aida*, had just been taken to the hospital for an emergency operation. He wondered whether Leontyne knew the part. She had no sooner told him that she did than she was rushed into preparations as a replacement for the ailing star.

Leontyne tried to compose herself by remembering that she was familiar with the score, or music. In addition, she knew that the conductor would make sure she could be heard. Still, it was her first leading role, and there was no time for a lot of rehearsal.

Making her final preparations, Leontyne calmly thought over her entrances and exits. Then, just before the performance, she realized that she couldn't remember the place on the stage where her character was supposed to die. Frantic, she rushed over to the director, who was busy checking the stage before the curtain went up. "Where am I going to die?" she blurted out. "I haven't the slightest idea where I'm going to die!" Everyone laughed, and Leontyne relaxed, too. And when she went onstage, her performance brought the usually cool, reserved San Francisco opera goers to their feet, applauding a new Aida.

After this performance, opportunities came one after another for Leontyne. Later that same year her manager asked her to come to Carnegie Hall, not telling her for whom she would be singing. A number of people were scattered thoughout the front rows of the empty hall. One, a slim, good-looking man with salt-and-pepper hair, was eating a club sandwich when she began to sing. Midway through the aria, or solo, from *Aida*, this man jumped up, pushed the musician who was accompanying Leontyne aside, and played the piano himself.

When she finished singing, he introduced himself as Herbert Von Karajan, director of the Vienna (Austria) State Opera. Leontyne's voice had given goose bumps to the usually stern, demanding Von Karajan. The conductor persuaded her to make her debut in Europe with the Vienna Opera the following year, 1958, in *Aida*. In that production, Von Karajan got an outstanding performance from his new discovery.

"I love, enjoy, and admire him," said Leontyne of Von Karajan. "I use notes I don't know I have when I sing with him. When he says I can do something, I believe I can do it."

From Vienna, Leontyne went to London for a triumphant production of *Aida* at Covent Garden, where she received one of the most enthusiastic responses ever given to an American singer. Applauded throughout her performance, she was cheered long after the last curtain.

Leontyne has had some of her greatest successes in Aida. *Here she performs the role in San Francisco in 1959. . .*

Following the London success, she received an offer from the La Scala opera house in Milan, Italy to star in Richard Strauss's *Salome.* After consulting with her manager, however, Leontyne decided to turn down the offer from this premier opera company. The role of Salome was not yet firmly in her repertoire (the roles she knew well), and there wasn't enough time to study it further right then. Leontyne decided instead to continue her European tour and to hope for another chance to

And again in 1984, when she sang her farewell at the Metropolitan Opera in New York.

perform at La Scala. In the meantime, she promised herself that she would not go to the famous brown brick La Scala theater as a tourist; she would wait until she was invited again to sing.

Leontyne did not have to wait long for a better offer. The next invitation from La Scala, to sing Aida, came in 1960. By then, she had made the role of the Ethiopian princess her own. The first black singer to appear in a principal role at La Scala, she made her debut there without a single stage rehearsal. Audience and reviewers alike took her to their hearts. The Milan writers praised her acting, singing, and appearance. Her voice, they said, was a marvel. Its power seemed to come with almost no effort, building from the softest murmur to tremendous volume. In a floor-length, one-strapped white gown that perfectly suited her, she moved like a princess on the huge stage.

Before the La Scala debut, Laurel, Mississippi celebrated the successes of its hometown girl by inviting her to sing at a benefit for St. Paul's Methodist Church, where her parents still worshipped. The whole town, black and white, turned out, sitting together to listen to its famous daughter.

"It was the sweetest thing that ever happened to me," Leontyne later said. "All those people have wished me well, prayed for me, gone out of their way to ask my mother about my work. It wasn't the best I've ever sung. I was too choked up emotionally. But I think that concert represented a great deal of progress for a little town in the Deep South. For an hour and a half, we weren't white or black; we were just human beings. In Laurel, I saw no hate or prejudice."

The Prices and the Chisholms shared the front row of the benefit and their pride in Leontyne's homecoming. "I feel that God has favored us more than most by allowing us to participate in Leontyne's career," reflected Mrs. Chisholm. "Our reward has been the fun—the privilege—of helping her when she needed it. I think someone with a talent like hers is one of God's chosen creatures."

Once again, Leontyne drew strength from her family and friends. Together with her remarkable talent, that strength gave her the confidence she exhibited on the great stage of La Scala. From her triumph in Milan, she went on to the Berlin Festival in Germany.

After Berlin, the Metropolitan Opera Company in New York City beckoned to Leontyne a second time with an offer from Rudolf Bing, its famous and terrifying director. When the Met had contacted Leontyne the first time, Florence Page Kimball had advised Leontyne to decline. A singer should have at least five roles in which she is outstanding before she accepted a Met contract, the voice coach had told her student. Leontyne had had mixed feelings about that first refusal. She worried that another offer might not come. Forgetting all that she had already accomplished all over the world, she was afraid the decision was foolish. When a second offer came, she found herself glad she had waited.

Leonora, in Verdi's *Il Trovatore*, was the role Leontyne sang for her 1961 Met debut. She felt perfectly at home as the Spanish noblewoman Leonora and poured herself into the singing. Although she would sing Aida later that season at the Met, she did not choose it for her debut, preferring not to appear first in a role often associated with black singers.

On the night of Leontyne's first appearance there, the Metropolitan Opera House was buzzing with excitement. Success in her own country as well as abroad had built Leontyne's reputation, and American opera goers were eager to welcome her to the most famous opera theater in the country.

Leontyne's years of study and work had prepared her for her big moment as a singer. But before the performance, she asked for help as she had since childhood. "Dear Jesus," she prayed, "you got me into this, now get me out."

During the performance, the audience interrupted with cheers of "Brava!"—the traditional accolade given a woman performer. At the end, the audience applauded for thirty-five minutes. It was Leontyne's night. Beyond the footlights, Mr. and Mrs. Price, George Price, the Chisholms and their three daughters, and Florence Page Kimball shared her joy.

William Warfield did not attend, but he sent his greetings. Warfield and Leontyne, who had lived separate professional lives for years, spent little time together. They had had no children. At the time of the Met debut they had formally separated, but did not get divorced until 1973.

During the intermission of *Il Trovatore* that first night, Rudolf Bing had asked Leontyne how she was doing. Leontyne replied, "Mr. Bing, I'm having a ball." That sense of fun continued late into the evening. At the opening night party after the performance she announced, "Nobody's going to leave this party unhappy." She went straight to the piano and sang "Summertime," everybody's favorite song from *Porgy and Bess*.

Following Florence Kimball's advice about five strong roles, Leontyne's first-year contract at the Met called for her to appear in four other roles that she had performed successfully elsewhere. That season she sang Donna Anna in *Don Giovanni*, Cio-Cio-San in *Madame Butterfly*, the title role of *Aida*, and Liu in *Turandot*. In that first year with them, she became a valuable member of the company. At the season's end, Rudolf Bing asked her to play the lead in the next year's opening night offering, *Girl of the Golden West* by Puccini. For the first time ever a black singer was scheduled to sing a principal role at a Metropolitan Opera House opening night.

Il Trovatore *was the opera in which Leontyne made her Metropolitan Opera debut. Here she portrays Leonora.*

The Met's 1961 opening was delayed by a musicians' strike that had to be settled by U.S. Secretary of Labor Arthur Goldberg. From Salzburg, Austria, where she was singing in the city's yearly opera festival, Leontyne followed news reports of the labor talks. When they were settled and the opening date announced, she sent a recording of Bach's "Goldberg Variations" to the secretary with a note of thanks.

As had been planned, Leontyne sang the lead role in *Girl of the Golden West* on opening night. Puccini's story is about a serious, reform-minded young woman named Minnie. The opera is set in the composer's idea of the American West, filled with cowboys and saloons. As with many operas, the beautiful music is more interesting than the story.

It is unusual for principal singers to appear in opening night roles that they haven't performed before. For Leontyne, it was a risk that she later regretted. Reflecting on the opening, she decided that the role did not suit her and she dropped it from her repertoire. Later that season, overwork and fatigue caught up with her. Her managers rearranged her schedule to allow her a short vacation in Rome, the first she'd ever taken.

Enjoying the city, she rented a small apartment near the Piazzo Venezia to which she retreated from time to time during the 1960s. After the brief pause, Leontyne returned to full-time singing at the Met. Between 1961 and 1969, she sang a total of 118 performances on the great stage and became a familiar well-loved figure at the opera house.

Arriving long before curtain time, she liked to set out her "trinkets" on the dressing room table: pictures of her parents, her brother and his children, and Herbert

Von Karajan, the conductor, as well as a little mascot dachshund that made her laugh. She brought from home a container of hot soup to sip before difficult scenes that made her feel tense.

Although Leontyne was described by one member of the opera house's staff as being not typical, by Met standards, because she was "too nice," she is demanding when necessary. She does not hesitate to show her temper when professional matters are the issue. Once, when told that another singer would miss a rehearsal, she was outraged. With his voice, she noted, he was lucky to appear with her and ought to do everything he could to improve his performance.

Her ranking at the Met was evident in 1966: Rudolf Bing selected her to sing the principal role for the season's opening in its new house at Lincoln Center for the Performing Arts. The new center contained separate buildings for the Metropolitan Opera House, Philharmonic Hall, a library, and the State Theater, which would become the permanent home of the New York City Opera Company.

To mark the opening of the new opera house, Samuel Barber had written a new opera, *Antony and Cleopatra*, and had written the role of Cleopatra with Leontyne's voice in mind. Franco Zefferelli was hired as the designer; he planned a magnificent stage production. Each part of the design became more and more elaborate. At some point, the basic element of opera, the singing, seemed to be overlooked. In fact, so much time was spent on rehearsing scenery changes that rehearsal of the music received little attention.

The elaborate production, most of which did not work as planned, created confusion both for the company and the audience. The only thing that the reviewers could find to praise was Leontyne's singing.

The disappointment of *Antony and Cleopatra* made Leontyne examine the support she was receiving from the Met's management. Despite the number of performances she had given, an average of more than thirteen in each of the eight seasons when she was one of the Met's leading singers, she appeared in only two new productions, including the ill-fated *Antony and Cleopatra*. Although there is a solid core of operas, and most singers perform a limited number of roles, new productions are exciting. Leontyne was disappointed that during the eight years at the Met, Rudolf Bing did little to expand her repertoire or offer her new productions. In 1969 she sang Aida twice and the following year did not appear at all. In the next two years, she rarely appeared at Lincoln Center.

During this time, she sang abroad and at the San Francisco Opera House, where she was offered new roles. Her guest appearances included debuts in Buenos Aires and Hamburg. She became more selective in signing Metropolitan Opera Company contracts, agreeing to perform in new roles or in new productions of her favorites. Between 1971 and the present time, she has paced herself differently. With fewer opera engagements, she was able to increase her concert appearances, a kind of singing that she always enjoyed. In addition, she recorded many of her famous roles. Without the commitments to long opera house seasons, she could enjoy life a little more. Knowing that her voice had a limited number of years, she chose to work it less hard.

Leontyne Price is respected by others in her profession as a gifted singer who works extremely hard. She spends enormous amounts of time learning the details of each role, believing that the singing is only one part of the total performance.

She takes pride in her black heritage, but expects to be accepted as an individual and as a singer, not as a representative of her race. Although she helped to break many racial barriers, Leontyne has concentrated on excelling in her profession. From the beginning of her career, when it was still unusual to see a black singer on an opera stage, she refused to disguise her skin color with makeup. (Her only exception is the chalklike makeup for Cio-Cio-San in *Madame Butterfly* that every singer uses.) Audiences have often seen her sing roles that only white singers once performed.

As an outstanding American singer, she has received many honors, including sixteen Grammy awards, the highest honor of the recording industry, awarded by the National Academy of Recording Arts and Sciences. Leontyne was the first opera star to receive the Presidential Medal of Freedom. Her 1979 television program, "Leontyne Price at the White House," won her an Emmy that year. She has sung for several presidents, honoring President Lyndon B. Johnson at his inauguration and again at his funeral. She has appeared several times at the White House, notably at ceremonies welcoming Pope John Paul II in 1979 and at the signing of the Egyptian-Israeli peace treaty that same year.

Musical America chose her as its "Musician of the Year" and *Harper's Bazaar* named her the "American Woman of Accomplishment." She was listed as one of "America's Most Important Women" by President Johnson and included in *Life* magazine's list of "Remarkable American Women, 1776-1976." For its "Gallery of Heroes," a list of men and women who reflect values worth celebrating, *Saturday Review* chose Leontyne, the only opera star so honored. A number of colleges and universities, including Dartmouth, Howard, Columbia, Yale, Harvard, Fordham and her own Central State, have awarded her honorary doctor of music degrees.

Leontyne has supported various projects in the arts: she has served as an advisory board member for Channel 13, the New York PBS station, and as a member of the Advisory Board of the National Cultural Center. Interested in helping the youth of New York City, she is a member of the Board of the Harlem School of Ballet and is an advisory member of the Dance Theater of Harlem. She is a trustee and member of the Board of Directors of International House, and vice-president of the Whitney M. Young, Jr., Memorial Foundation.

Between trips abroad, Leontyne still lives alone in her dollhouse-like home on a quiet street in New York City's Greenwich Village. She and William Warfield bought the house while they were still married. It is furnished with eighteenth-century French furniture bought on her trips to Europe, and has a blue and green color scheme. The study, where she learns her music and answers mail, overlooks a beautiful garden. In this house she entertains friends, sometimes preparing for them her mother's recipe for shrimp gumbo or perhaps luscious Italian food.

On January 3, 1985, Leontyne appeared in her last opera performance as Aida at the Metropolitan Opera House. In a twenty-five-minute ovation, the audience bid her farewell in a shower of flowers and confetti. Ending this one phase of her career, she will continue to sing in concerts and will have time to be what she calls "just Leontyne." "Just Leontyne" is at heart a calm, steady person. With friends her reserved but self-confident manner gives way to warmth and humor.

She has never forgotten her heritage: the two grandfathers who were Methodist ministers, and the parents who loved her, helping to shape the person she became. To them she owes her strong character and the deep religious faith that has sustained her during times of stress and discouragement.

Determination and hard work helped to make her a success. She has always been a willing student, able to accept correction and advice from those whom she respected. Along the way, she expressed her gratitude to family, friends, and those in her field who supported and helped her.

Leontyne is most thankful for the gift of her voice. Joyfully, she has shared it with the world.

PLAYING THROUGH

DYLANA JENSON: A prodigy who began studying violin at age three, this woman played with symphony orchestras, on television, and in a famous international competition before she was out of her teens.

On the evening of July 27, 1972, almost every TV set in tiny Costa Rica was turned to Channel 7. The date marked the first concert of the National Symphony Orchestra to be shown live on television. The audience knew that the guest artist, Dylana Jenson, was only eleven years old. For weeks before, everyone in the Central American country had heard about the young American girl. She was going to play one of the most difficult pieces of music for the violin, Peter Tchaikovsky's Concerto in D Major.

On the stage of the packed National Theater, Dylana looked like any other sixth grader dressed up for a special occasion. Her mother had made the short, white dress she wore. Tall for her age, Dylana wore knee-length white socks which made her legs look even longer. Her shiny brown hair was neatly parted and brushed back into a single thick braid.

She tuned her violin and then stood still, waiting. At conductor Gerald Brown's signal, the orchestra began the slow introduction to the solo section of the concerto. Then Dylana began to play. Skilfully drawing her bow across the violin's thin strings, she filled the hushed hall with lovely music.

When she finished, the applause was deafening. A procession of children approached the stage, carrying flowers. Even the musicians stood to join in the applause. After the fourth curtain call, the audience's clapping became rhythmic. Keeping time together, hands and feet pounded as one, while the great hall almost shook with the sound.

Surprised and pleased, Dylana bowed and smiled, holding a bouquet of flowers in her arms. The conductor turned suddenly and bent to whisper in her ear. An encore? They wanted her to play another piece? So that was what the rhythmic clapping meant! She laughed with delight, and putting down the flowers, picked up her violin once more. This time she played a piece all by herself, while the orchestra members listened along with the audience.

Standing backstage with her parents, Dylana accepted the congratulations of family friends. Everyone was curious to know how this young girl had become such a skilled musician. She had arrived in Costa Rica a few days before. Since then, they had watched her laughing and playing games with her cousins. Seeing her with the other children, no one could have guessed at her unusual talent.

For Dylana, playing the violin was not unusual. She could not remember a time when she did not play her instrument. It was as natural to her as speaking. How many people remember learning to speak?

The story of Dylana Jenson's musical ability is actually the story of a special family. Dylana's parents held strong beliefs about raising children. They thought every child should discover and develop some particular artistic interest. As a result, their home had a room filled with musical instruments, paints, and clay. Each of their six children was encouraged to experiment with these things.

All of the children had some special interest. Dylana's sisters Pamela and Vicky spent their days drawing. Her older brother Peter had fish tanks and diving equipment. In addition, he played the cello. Kevan, who was two years older than Dylana, also wanted to play that instrument.

Dylana was the fifth child. Born on May 14, 1961 in Sherman Oaks, California, near Los Angeles, she was named for her father's favorite poet, Dylan Thomas. A happy little girl, she walked when she was only nine months old.

The house was filled with music. When she was very young, Dylana knew the sound of certain pieces by heart. Kevan had learned to operate the record player when he was eighteen months old. His favorite record, Dmitri Shostakovich's Fifth Symphony, was familiar to the whole family, and he often replayed a particular part.

One day, Kevan and Dylana built a huge structure with building blocks that suddenly toppled, burying her in the middle. Her screams brought Mrs. Jenson running to pick up the frightened ten month old. In the background, Kevan's favorite part of the symphony record sounded. Suddenly, Dylana's cries stopped, as she waited for the expected crash of cymbals. As soon as their sound faded away, she began to howl once more.

At first it seemed that Dylana would not turn to any particular form of music or art. She watched Vicky draw and stared at Kevan as he struggled with his cello. But she was happy just being a two year old. She seemed content to follow her mother as she took care of baby Ivan. While the other children were noted for their activities, she was called "Dylana the Beautiful." This soon was shortened to "Lanny Boo," which remained her nickname.

In any other family, of course, Dylana would not have been unusual. But the Jensons were not an ordinary family. At the age of two and a half or three, the older children had already begun a fierce concentration on their area of interest. Kevan's early fascination with listening to music had prompted a strong desire in him to perform.

Mr. and Mrs. Jenson wanted to help him with his cello. By the age of five, Kevan had worked with several string teachers. They had taught him to count and name the notes. He could play a scale and hold the bow correctly. But none of this helped him to play even the short pieces that he had heard and loved. No one knew how to teach such a very small child.

One day the Jensons heard that Dr. Shinichi Suzuki was coming to Los Angeles. He was a famous Japanese teacher who had developed a remarkable new approach to music instruction. Little children in the Suzuki group were playing finished pieces of music with ease and enjoyment soon after beginning lessons.

Dr. Suzuki helped children learn the violin in the same way that they learned to speak their own language.

Dylana didn't seem interested in any one art at first, but at age two and a half she started playing the violin.

He encouraged them to imitate the music they heard. With help, the students discovered a new skill to be learned while playing each piece. Then the piece was learned from memory. The quality of performing is most important in Suzuki instruction, not the speed of learning. Suzuki's songs appealed to a child's sense of play and need to move about.

Watching a demonstration of the Suzuki method, Ana Jenson knew that at last she would be able to help Kevan. Her husband bought Kevan a tiny violin, one-eighth the size of an adult instrument. When Dylana saw it, she asked for one, too. And so Lee Jenson purchased another violin for her and Vicky to share.

At the time, there was no Suzuki workshop in Los Angeles. A friend who offered to teach the children lived too far away. Ana decided that it would be easier for her to teach them herself. She bought an adult-size violin and a Suzuki book. Almost immediately, she discovered that daily, not weekly lessons, were needed. Each night, she would learn the lessons that she would teach the children the next day.

Kevan was terribly eager to succeed, but he did not have the patience needed to perfect each step. Vicky soon lost interest and returned to her drawing. But little Dylana was a natural student. She rarely put the violin down. Holding it as she rode her tricycle, she trailed after her brothers and sisters. Later, when she went to kindergarten, she took the violin with her. At "Show and Tell" time, she played it for her classmates.

Ana taught her daughter to master each small step, showing her where to place her hands. At no time did Dylana imagine that anything was too difficult, nor did she learn mistakes that had to be corrected. Instead of practicing separate exercises, she started with short, easy, but very beautiful pieces of music. When she learned "The Happy Farmer," she and Ana danced around, imitating a happy farmer. The lessons and practice became part of the normal routine of the Jenson house. Everyone learned to speak louder to be heard above the violin that played in the background.

By the time Dylana was four years old, Ana could no longer keep up with her. She was already playing a concerto, the first major piece that Suzuki students learned when quite advanced. When Dr. Suzuki returned to Los Angeles that year, Dylana played a Vivaldi concerto for him. Delighted, he encouraged the Jensons to develop her talent fully.

Ana had heard of an excellent teacher in Los Angeles, Eunice Wennermark. As soon as they met, Ana knew that she had found the right person for Dylana. A cheerful, friendly woman, Wennermark was full of energy. She could see how effective Ana's teaching was and she agreed to follow the same procedure. There was no need to teach scales to this young musician, she could see.

The Jensons had not intended to develop a prodigy, a child whose musical ability was years ahead of her age. For them, it seemed perfectly natural that Dylana loved music and performed it well. Not until she started school did they seek more expert advice.

Through a friend, Lee contacted someone who knew the famous violinist, Jascha Heifetz. Dylana remembers her conversation with Heifetz. "My voice was squeaky because I had just had my tonsils out, and he said he had them out when he was about my age and the best thing about it was all the ice cream he got."

Impressed with her ability, Heifetz agreed to accept

her as a student. To begin, he assigned her to an assistant
for two lessons each week. Heifetz himself planned to see
her every four or five weeks.

It seemed like a wonderful opportunity until Ana
Jenson observed the first two lessons with the assistant.
Her approach was totally different from Suzuki's. The
assistant told Dylana that she should stop listening to
records. She must learn to develop her own sound, without any influence from other artists.

Ana and Lee disagreed with this woman. They were
convinced that no one was born knowing how the different styles of music should sound. They believed people
learned music by listening to it. Dylana had always listened to many famous violinists playing the same piece.
Learning that one piece could have many approaches,
she would try to discover her own way to play it.

The Jensons were unwilling to turn their daughter
over to someone, no matter how highly recommended,
with whom they differed so much. It was not an easy
decision to give up the contact with Heifetz. In time, they
knew, he might suggest other opportunities. But the Jensons did what they felt was best for Dylana and her love
of music.

They decided to look for a teacher who recognized
Dylana's learning style and agreed with their deeply held
beliefs. Eventually they turned to Manuel Compinsky.
He was well known as a superb master violin teacher, and
was also a warm human being. Often, he scheduled extra
lessons each week with Dylana, for which he refused
payment. At the same time, Anita Swearengin, a family
friend and pianist, worked with Dylana as an accompanist and coach. In competitions sponsored by the American String Teachers of Los Angeles, Dylana won first

Manuel Compinsky was Dylana's teacher when she was younger. He saw so much talent in Dylana that he often scheduled extra lessons for free.

prize awards. The awards helped pay for the mounting costs of her studies.

While in second grade at the Gester Avenue School, Dylana served as the concertmistress, or leader, of the student orchestra. A top student, she took part in a special program for gifted and talented children. By the time she was in the third grade, though, her mother recognized that she needed more time for lessons and practice. Her school administrators agreed to have Dylana's school day end at noon.

Dylana began to perform in public at concerts near home when she was still a little girl. One weekend afternoon in 1968, she played a Bach concerto at a college in Beverly Hills. After the performance, the famous comedian Jack Benny came up to meet her. Many people enjoyed the jokes he made about his violin playing, but few of them knew that in his spare time he was a serious musician.

Benny invited Dylana to play the D Minor Concerto for Two Violins by J. S. Bach with him in his office. Later his sense of fun led to them playing a violin duet on television. The cheerful seven year old played with her clear, true sound, while Benny tried to keep up in the comic style loved by his fans.

Having Dylana appear on Jack Benny's show was fun. However, the Jensons turned down an offer for her to repeat the performance in Las Vegas. She was developing as a prodigy, they knew, but they were not interested in displaying her as a curiosity or an oddity.

When David Oistrakh, the Russian violinist, heard Dylana the next year, he said firmly, "She has everything to be a great violinist." He immediately called his manager, Sol Hurok, who offered to represent her. Hurok promised a slow, carefully prepared development, with only two or three events each year. Nothing would be rushed. However, while the Jensons were still considering his offer, the great manager died.

The interview with Oistrakh and Hurok prompted Lee Jenson to call Alberto Bolet, the conductor of the Long Beach Symphony. He was willing to have Dylana play for him. As a result, in 1969 she was invited to perform a violin solo with the Long Beach Symphony. Seven thousand people attended the concert. In the next few years, Lee arranged other performances for his daughter, acting as her manager and booking agent.

When Dylana was invited to appear on Merv Griffin's TV talk show, Lee prepared a press release that quoted reviews of her performances. Ana, who was from Costa Rica, sent a copy of the release to a TV station in that country. A childhood friend of hers, Guido Saenz, heard the announcement on a news program. Saenz, who was Vice Minister of Culture, was planning the following season of the National Symphony. He invited Dylana to open the season as a solo performer.

After the televised performance, she was an overnight sensation in Costa Rica. She was asked to remain and give another program the following week. It, too, was completely sold out. At the Grand Hotel, across the square from the National Theater, the Jensons' rooms were filled with flowers. Everywhere the family went, people recognized Dylana and greeted her. On trips to the countryside, at the volcanoes, and in the market places, she was instantly surrounded. She left Costa Rica with her first taste of the tremendous joy her music brought to other people.

The 1972 concert in Costa Rica was a turning point

in Dylana's life as a prodigy. Four performances with the Seattle Symphony followed during the 1972-73 concert season. Appearing at the General Assembly of the Organization of American States in Washington, D.C., she received glowing reviews. At Jack Benny's recommendation, conductor Andre Kostelanetz invited her to perform in three New York Philharmonic "Promenades" concerts at Lincoln Center in New York City. The manager of the orchestra told the Associated Press that she was the best young violinist that they had ever seen or worked with.

Dylana's tour had lasted three weeks. Upon returning to junior high school in Van Nuys, California, she learned how much school work she had missed. She wanted to catch up with the class before leaving for her return engagement in Costa Rica in June. Worried about falling further behind, she stayed up late at night to study. It was the first time that schoolwork had been a problem.

From Costa Rica, Dylana went to El Salvador for two more concerts. In July she enrolled in a two-week master class in Zurich, Switzerland with the noted violinist Nathan Milstein. Milstein urged Dylana to concentrate totally on developing her talent. The next few years were important, he believed, if she really wanted a career as a solo violinist. He himself had left school at an early age to concentrate on his music.

There were a number of reasons why it would be possible for Dylana to stop going to school. Ana had been a teacher, and Lee was working towards a doctor's degree in literature. Their home was always alive with discussions. And when Dylana didn't have her violin, she was reading. With her upcoming tours, she would learn geography and international studies in the best possible way, by experience.

The young violinist played many concerts with the National Symphony of Costa Rica.

At first Dylana couldn't imagine what it would be like to leave school. Yet, she had been so busy for the last few years that none of her classmates were really close friends. In fact, her best friends were her brothers and sisters. In addition, she remembered how difficult it had been to catch up with the seventh grade after her spring tour. The coming concert season would be even busier.

After the Jensons decided to take Dylana out of school, she never missed it. Ivan, Vicky, and Kevan brought their friends home and told her everything that was going on. She knew what she had to learn by following their studies. When she had difficulty understanding something, her father or mother helped.

Even before she left school, a great deal of Dylana's education occurred outside the classroom. Discussions of current events took place every day at home. When Dr. Martin Luther King was shot in 1968, the Jenson family shared the shock and sorrow of other Americans. Yet they knew that people who had looked to Dr. King as their social leader had a greater sorrow. Wanting to offer their sympathy in more than words, they went to a church service in Watts, the black section of Los Angeles. There, Dylana came to understand how important Dr. King's work had been.

Her European recital debut, arranged by Milstein, took place during the 1972-73 season. In a recital, the solo musician performs without an orchestra, accompanied only by a pianist. The program is chosen to represent all the important periods of music, and usually includes one long show piece, something that the musician can play extremely well. It requires careful preparation, with attention to the smallest detail. Except for the accompanist, the musician is alone for the lengthy program.

Each year for the next three years, Dylana toured Europe, with concerts in Switzerland, France, and Germany. At home between tours, she practiced and read. Like many young people, she was concerned about the environment, and wrote letters that supported efforts to save the whales. Following the advice of her friend and teacher, Manuel Compinsky, she kept fit by jogging and riding her bicycle. Careful about her diet, she developed a taste for health foods. In her spare time, she crocheted baby clothes for her sister Pamela's little boy.

Nearly fourteen years old now, Dylana began more and more to discover things in the music by herself. Her practice became something she did alone to sort out her feelings about what she was learning. In addition, her work with Nathan Milstein had made her aware of the special sound of her music she wanted to develop.

Her frequent appearances with orchestras throughout the United States and Europe attracted the attention of managers and booking agents who arranged concerts. Many of them who offered to represent Dylana wanted to arrange tours of major cities. The Jensons knew that a good manager, who had contacts with top orchestras, could help, but they were concerned about Dylana's development as an artist. They declined the offers, preferring to direct their daughter's career themselves. That way, she would not be rushed into anything before she was ready.

In 1976 the Jensons moved to Bloomington, Indiana. There, between concert tours, Dylana could play for Josef Gingold, a professor of music at Indiana University. In the small college town, Dylana made friends with other musicians. Unlike Los Angeles, where the few violin students she knew were hours away, here she lived

close to everyone. Mr. and Mrs. Jenson welcomed Dylana's friends from the university into their home, took
them ice skating, and included them on family picnics.
Although they were a few years older, the music students
felt at home with Dylana, Ivan, Vicky, and their friends.

While the Jensons lived in Bloomington, Dylana
continued to appear with the National Symphony of
Costa Rica. Her appearances with the orchestra had
made her a symbol of the new interest in culture in that
country. The concerts had aroused national pride and
renewed attention to music. Local groups began performing together. The Youth Orchestra became popular, and
record numbers of children signed up for music lessons.
Attendance at the symphony climbed.

In gratitude, the Costa Rican government made
Dylana an honorary citizen in May, 1976. It also appointed Ana to a position with the United Nations, repre-
senting the arts of Costa Rica. While traveling with her
daughter, her job was to spread the news of the artistic life
of her native country. She also attended United Nations
committee meetings.

Although this support made Dylana's lessons and
many other expenses possible, the young musician
longed to help. She wanted to be able to support herself
with her music. Aware of her parents' sacrifices for her,
she looked forward to a time when she would not have to
rely on their help. Also, she wanted to begin helping her
brothers and sisters.

Like Dylana, her friends in Bloomington also
longed to be self-supporting. They talked endlessly of
getting the "big break." Some of them thought about
entering the Tchaikovsky Competition. This important
music contest is held every four years in Moscow, in the

Soviet Union. An international event, the four-week long competition attracts worldwide attention.

In the first Tchaikovsky Competition held in 1958, Van Cliburn, a young pianist from Texas, won first prize. Overnight, he became the most popular musician in the United States. Sought after for concert and recital engagements, Cliburn was a frequent guest on television talk shows.

Dylana's friends envied Cliburn's success. They hoped that someday they would be ready for the Tchaikovsky Competition. Listening to them, Dylana wondered whether she should enter the next event. She would be just seventeen years old at the time.

Nathan Milstein was surprised at his student's interest in the competition. Those who entered were usually older, in their twenties, and were fairly well known. He warned Dylana that first place winners got all the glory; no one seemed to remember the others.

Still, the idea appealed to her. Josef Gingold would represent the United States on the jury. One of his students, a young violinist from Iran, was also going.

On the plane trip to Moscow in 1978, Dylana had some doubts that she had made the right decision; her preparations had been slowed by many difficulties. Because she was not a student at the university, she had difficulty finding a suitable pianist in Bloomington with whom to work. Then, two months before the date, she came down with pneumonia and had to spend three weeks in bed. Fortunately, a retired professor at the university had been able to give her some help. But she only had had time to rehearse the first pieces in her program and to perform them once in a recital the day before she left.

In contrast, the other American musicians had spent months in careful preparation. She overheard one young man say, "I gave eleven recitals this year on this material." Another had performed parts of the program sixteen times. And Dylana had performed it in recital once!

In Moscow she discovered that the Russians had worked even harder. A Russian woman described the help they received from the government. "We were trained like Olympic sportsmen," she said. "We went where there were many cottages—trees, beautiful country. We just played and rested. Then we played every program three, four, five times in different cities and towns."

Nevertheless, Dylana's decision to come had been her own, and she was determined to do her best. She prepared the music for each round as it came up, working with the accompanist provided by her hosts. In order to hear as much music as she could, she went to all the performances. It was fun to meet so many gifted young people who came to the famous event from all over the world. The musicians were assigned rooms in the Rossiya, the world's largest hotel, located across Red Square from the Kremlin.

As each round ended, those who did not win went home, until only the finalists remained. On the night of the final round, Dylana and her mother rode the special bus to the Great Hall of the Moscow Conservatory. Inside the stone entrance, with its tall columns, competition posters covered the walls.

In the packed hall were some other United States musicians who had come to cheer for Dylana, the last performer in the competition. Already, the Americans had won a first prize gold medal for cello. Another American violinist, Elmar Oliveira, who had also reached the final round, had been outstanding the night before. In this round, contestants played the Tchaikovsky Concerto and another concerto of their choice.

Waiting her turn backstage, Dylana was surprised at how little applause the Russians gave their favorite violinist, Ilya Grubert. In contrast, tremendous applause followed Dylana's first piece, the Sibelius Concerto. Even after the three-minute rest period between pieces, it did not end. Finally, after many minutes, Dylana could come out to play the Tchaikovsky Concerto.

In the pause after the first movement of the concerto, the audience, disobeying the rule of waiting until the end, broke into applause. When she finished the concerto, they cheered wildly, crying, "Brava!" The applause thundered, and then became rhythmic. Chants of "First prize! First prize!" did not stop, even when the lights were flicked on and off. When the lights were turned off completely, the audience stayed, clapping in the dark.

The entire orchestra came backstage in a rare tribute, lining up in single file to congratulate her. Forty-five minutes later, when she stepped outside the theater, hundreds of people cried together, "Brava!" In the glare of the TV lights, she signed autographs while a bystander observed, "I was here twenty years ago when Cliburn played. . . .It is the same now."

Yet the next day, Grubert was chosen to share the first prize gold medal with Elmar Oliveira! Since he had played brilliantly, Oliveira's success was no surprise. But the judges' decision to place Grubert above Dylana shocked everyone. She shared second prize with a violinist from Roumania. In fact, each of the four prizes

Even though Dylana played beautifully in the final round of the Tchaikovsky Competition, she placed second.

awarded for violin was shared with a musician from a Communist country. Of the twelve finalists in the violin division in 1978, eight of them received awards.

Dylana was amazed that politics would change the results of a music competition. Until then, she had believed that the best performers always won. A reporter who called to interview her was surprised by the strong-willed, independent young woman who said exactly what she thought about the results of the contest.

Dylana received a silver medal and a cash award. She also accepted an invitation to return for a recital tour of the six biggest cities of the Soviet Union. When she made the tour, it was sold out many weeks in advance. But back home, offers of concert engagements did not come. Exhausted from the strains of the competition and the tour, Dylana was discouraged. Later, she talked about her feelings.

"Yes, I was upset at the end of the competition, and said so. I was shocked and upset, not because I didn't win, but because of the whole experience. . . . It suddenly dawned on me: other things were involved here besides the music.

"That was my coming of age. I didn't perform for eleven months afterward."

After the competition, Dylana moved with her family to New Rochelle, near New York City. For the first time in her life, she stopped playing the violin. Not until the following March, when she was invited to play with the National Symphony of Costa Rica, did she begin to practice again. By then, a New York manager had contacted her, and the future brightened.

First, RCA signed her for a recording contract. Then, she was invited to perform with conductor Eugene

Ormandy and the Philadelphia Orchestra in Carnegie Hall, New York City, in December 1980. The performance, her first with a major orchestra in this country since the competition, was televised nationally. Ormandy complimented Dylana on "her nerves of steel." The New York events formed a triple debut: Carnegie Hall, national television, and an RCA recording. (Her first RCA record, released in 1981, was with Ormandy and the Philadelphia Orchestra.) The music reviewer of the *New York Times* called Dylana "a mature musician."

Dylana's recital, or solo, debut at Carnegie Hall, another significant event in her career, followed the next year. Since then, she has appeared with major orchestras in Cleveland, Los Angeles, and Paris. She has also recorded the Sonatas for Violin and Piano by Johannes Brahms. Each year, she returns to Costa Rica to teach master classes for two weeks. Dylana is making her own decisions now, selecting programs and events. She no longer studies with a teacher, but works alone, perfecting the special sound of her music.

While performing with the Denver Symphony Orchestra in October, 1982, she met a cellist and composer whom she knew was a very special person. The following January, she and David Lockington became engaged. They were married on March 24, 1983. Soon afterward, David was appointed assistant conductor of the Denver Symphony Orchestra.

Dylana's concern for the environment continues. In Denver and on tour, she performs with David and a pianist in concerts that benefit Greenpeace. This organization, an outgrowth of the "save the whales" movement, is dedicated to peace and environmental issues.

The former child prodigy has developed into a mature musician. "Children can absorb an incredible amount," says Dylana. "When they are young, they can do anything when properly trained. It's true that many child prodigies don't make it to maturity [as musicians]. The problem is, too many of them won't or can't take the next step when they are older—becoming more independent and objective, as they should be, as they *must* be."

Dylana seems to be one prodigy who took that step. Although her life continues to be centered around her work, she can look beyond it. "I want to remain open to as many things as possible," she says. "After all, your music is a reflection of what you are."

Other Outstanding Women

MARIAN ANDERSON (1902-   ). Anderson has been singing since she was a child, first in her church choir and later in solo performances at churches and clubs. In 1925, a competition she won led to guest appearances with the New York Philharmonic Orchestra and the Philadelphia Orchestra, which were enthusiastically reviewed. Limited opportunities for black singers in the United States sent her to Europe in the 1930s, where she became celebrated for her rich voice with its unusual range. In Paris, Sol Hurok heard her and took over the management of her career. After an outstanding concert at Town Hall in 1935, she toured the United States and was heard by millions over major network radio programs. In 1955, Anderson became the first black singer to sing a major role at the Metropolitan Opera House. She continued her career as a concert singer until 1967, pausing only to serve for two years as the United States delegate to the United Nations. A gifted artist and a dignified, confident person, she helped remove barriers in the United States for many black musicians who followed her.

MRS. H.H.A. BEACH (1867-1944). An American composer and pianist who was born Amy Marcy Cheney, she used exclusively the name of Mrs. H.H.A. Beach after her marriage in 1885 to a Boston surgeon. A prodigy who had little formal instruction in music theory, she composed piano music and gave recitals of her pieces from the age of seven. At eighteen she married Dr. Beach and, with his encouragement, concentrated on composition. In that year she began her Mass in E Flat, which took three years to complete. Her most important work for orchestra was the "Gaelic Symphony," based on Gaelic folk tunes, and composed in 1896. She also wrote over one hundred and fifty songs. After her husband's death in 1910, Beach toured Europe, performing her works for piano. Back in the United States, she performed in concerts for the next twenty-five years. Although all but three of her compositions were published, she was not well known in her later years. However, current evaluation of Beach's compositions rank her among the leading musicians of the early twentieth century.

CARLA BLEY (1939-   ). The daughter of a piano teacher and a church organist in Oakland, California, composer Carla Bley's first exposure to music was in church. Early in life, she was attracted to black spirituals and jazz. At the age of fifteen, she left high school and went to New York. Working at odd jobs, she composed music for jazz singers and married Canadian pianist Paul Bley. She alternated composing with work as a cocktail waitress in Catskill Mountain resort hotels. After a second marriage and the birth of a daughter, Bley re-examined the music she was writing. Influenced by the Beatles, she moved away from the church spiritual and jazz sounds of her earlier work. She has since written longer, more complex music for full orchestra that is part of a new generation of jazz. Her current work brings together the different sounds heard in off-beat jazz, beer hall songs, electric rock, Italian opera, and church hymns. The most ambitious work is a two-hour-long opera, *Escalator Over the Hill*, scored for many instruments, including a Moog synthesizer and a calliope.

SARAH CALDWELL (1924-   ). The first woman to conduct at the Metropolitan Opera House in New York, Sarah Caldwell is doubly famous. Not only a renowned guest conductor, she is also producer and artistic director of the Opera Company of Boston. Born in Missouri and raised in Arkansas, she began her musical education by learning the violin. Graduating from high school at the age of fourteen, she entered the University of Arkansas, but left to study music. A scholarship to Northeastern Conservatory of Music brought her to Boston where she studied various instruments, conducting, opera production, and stage design. On another scholarship, she staged her first opera production at the Berkshire Music Festival (Tanglewood) in Marlboro, Massachusetts. The production won her a place in the festival's opera department and the chance to study with impresario Boris Goldovsky. As Goldovsky's assistant with the New England Opera Theater in Boston for ten years, she learned every phase of opera production. Caldwell's high standards of taste and elegance became a hallmark of her opera productions.

JUDY COLLINS (1939-   ). Born in Seattle, Washington, Judy Collins began studying the piano when she was four years old. In Denver, Colorado, Judy studied classical piano for eight years with master teacher and conductor Antonia Brico. As a teenager, she gave up the piano and learned the guitar, to accompany songs she wrote. During the folk music revival of the 1950s, she sang and played in local folk clubs. Collins was attracted to both the poetry of folk music and its musical forms. She made her first recording of folk songs in the early 1960s. Politically active during that time, she worked for black voter registration in Mississippi and joined the Women's Strike for Peace. Her original songs, several written for singer Joni Mitchell, sold many records. Collins published the *Judy Collins Songbook*, with words and music of her favorite songs and narrative sections that recall memories of her family and childhood. In 1974, she produced an award-winning documentary film about the life of her former teacher, *Antonia: A Portrait of the Woman*. Collins' music, in recent club and concert appearances and in her latest record albums, combines Broadway show tunes, folk, and modern music.

VIVIAN FINE (1913-   ). Early interest in music led Fine to demand and get piano lessons at the age of five. The following year, she began a three-year study, on a scholarship, at the Chicago Musical College. From 1924 to 1931 she worked with Djane Lavoie-Herz, and at her studio met most of the musicians experimenting with the new forms of music. Beginning in 1925, she studied harmony and composition with Ruth Crawford Seeger for four years. Seeger's encouragement was an important factor in her development. As a teenager, Fine wrote modern music for oboe, flute and piano. Her work was performed by groups in New York and Europe before she was twenty years old. Coming to New York in 1931 to study further, she began a second phase as a composer, creating music for dance. Fine has served on the music faculty of New York University and the Juilliard School of Music. Since 1964, she has taught at Bennington College. Her full-length opera, *The Women in the Garden*, is about a meeting of four women: Emily Dickinson, Isadora Duncan, Gertrude Stein, and Virginia Woolf.

CAROL FOX (1926-1982). With energy and enthusiasm, Carol Fox brought opera back to Chicago in 1952. (The city's last opera company had folded in 1932.) The only child of well-to-do parents, Fox had studied singing and acting in Chicago, California, and New York before beginning two years of voice and language study in Italy. She returned to the United States and, with her father's financial backing and the help of a business manager and a conductor, founded a new opera company. In 1956, the company became known as the Chicago Lyric Opera, and Fox became its general manager. For the next twenty-six years, she guided the company's artistic development while skillfully building its financial base. Responding to public tastes, Fox concentrated on presenting classic operas with European artists. Gradually she introduced unfamiliar works, while an apprentice program that she started trained young American singers. She died in 1982 after retiring, but left behind an internationally respected opera company.

MAUDE POWELL (1869-1920). Born in Peru, Illinois, Maude Powell began taking violin lessons from her mother at the age of four. By the time she was eight, she was performing Mozart violin sonatas in concert. She studied violin in Chicago until she was twelve, when the townspeople of Aurora, where she lived, sponsored her for a year of study in Europe. At fifteen, Powell began her adult concert career in London. After her European debut in 1885, she returned to the United States. Discouraged by the prejudice against female solo performers at the time, she formed the Maude Powell Quartet, which performed in the United States for four years. Later, she returned to Europe and toured Russia in 1903 with the John Philip Sousa Band. The following year, she married her English manager, H. Godfried Turner. When not on tour, Powell and her husband made their home in the United States. Powell introduced many violin concertos to the United States, and was one of the first violinists to perform the difficult Tchaikovsky Concerto in this country.

RISE STEVENS (1913-   ). Glamorous Rise Stevens brought opera to millions who enjoyed her performances on radio and in films during the early 1940s. Her debut at the Metropolitan Opera House in 1939 was followed a year later by her first appearance with the San Francisco Opera. In her first screen appearance, Stevens starred with Nelson Eddy in 1941 in *The Chocolate Soldier*, a film of the Victor Herbert operetta. In the popular movie, *Going My Way*, she sang the "Habanera" song from *Carmen*. Stevens' career as a singer began when she was ten years old, on "The Children's Hour" radio program. After graduating from high school, she performed for two years with the Opera-Comique in New York, then supported herself by singing in churches and on a radio show while she studied at Juilliard. During her summers, she studied in Salzburg, Germany. Discovered by George Szell, then conductor of the Prague Opera, she made her opera debut in Prague, Czechoslovakia in 1936, in *Mignon*. After her retirement from the Metropolitan Opera

Stevens shared her talent and experience with young musicians as a teacher.

EUGENIA ZUKERMAN (1944-   ). When she was a young girl, Eugenia Zukerman did not imagine herself as a solo musician. She had played the flute since she was ten years old, but as a teenager thought she would become a writer. Today she is one of a handful of renowned solo flute performers and has appeared with flautists Jean-Pierre Rampal and James Galway and with small groups. While her performing career was developing, she began to write again. Her novel about a young musician, *Deceptive Cadence* , was published in 1981. She also comments on music on the "CBS Sunday Morning." TV program. Eugenia is seriously pursuing each of her dual careers. Every day, when she is not on tour, Zukerman works in her studio, alternating flute practice with writing. Each activity stimulates the other, she says. "I'm terrifically happy when I'm going full steam and able to do a number of things."

Suggested Reading

Baggelaar, Kristin and Donald Milton. *Folk Song, More Than a Song.* New York: Thomas Y Crowell, 1976. Short biographies of leading folk singers highlight individual styles and list titles of songs for which each is famous.

Ewen, David. *Opera: Its Story Told Through the Lives and Works of its Foremost Composers.* New York: Franklin Watts, 1972. A complete source book, this volume contains the stories of the best-known operas, outlines the history of opera, and discusses different kinds of operas and types of voices.

Jackson, Jesse. *Make a Joyful Noise Unto the Lord!* New York: Thomas Y Crowell, 1974. Mahalia Jackson's gospel singing is traced from a New Orleans choir and the storefront churches of Chicago to the Lincoln Memorial where she sang for the Freedom Marchers in 1963.

Seeger, Ruth Crawford. *American Folk Songs For Children.* New York: Doubleday, 1948. Prefacing a collection of ninety songs, Seeger tells how to sing them, making use of rhythm, repetition, and humor, and recounts the story of how the book was created with her own children.

Seligmann, Jean and Juliet Danziger. *The Meaning of Music: The Young Listeners Guide.* Minneapolis: World Publishing Inc., 1966. Clear explanations of music theory and concepts make it easy to understand and enjoy the music of the past and present.

Shay, Arthur. *What It's Like to be a Musician.* Chicago: Reilly and Lee Books, 1972. While this photo story of guitarist Phil Upchurch follows him from rehearsals and performances to his home, it records his thoughts about his life and career.

Sills, Beverly. *Bubbles: A Self-Portrait.* Indianapolis: Bobbs-Merrill, 1976. Beverly Sills' own story of becoming an opera singer and her success with the New York City Opera is told with good humor and an appreciation of family, friends, and musicians.

Index

Catherine Scheader, who is both a writer and an educator, describes her involvement in music as that of an "audience." She feels strongly, though, that children who love music should be encouraged to pursue it. "Children need role models in music. Interest in a career in performing is often discouraged; some young musicians get boosts from their families, but many others don't. Gifted youngsters need to know that there are often people willing to guide them in developing their talents."

Ms. Scheader has had interest in many forms of art throughout her life. This book is not her first about artists; she earlier published biographies of painter Mary Cassatt and writer Lorraine Hansberry. While she was a classroom teacher, she tried to involve children in good art, music, and writing, because she feels the arts are a necessary part of learning.

Currently, Ms. Scheader supervises the reading and writing programs of an elementary school system in New Jersey, where she lives.

WITHDRAWN

**No longer the property of the
Boston Public Library.
Sale of this material benefits the Library.**